# B.C. Provincial Police Stories

Volume Two

by **CECIL CLARK**

The Kitwancool totem
in Victoria's Thunderbird
Park could also be
called the $64,000 totem.
(See page 78.)

Cecil Clark, far left, with Colin S. Campbell who prevented a possible lynching in "On the Trail of the Canton Giant" and helped solve the mystery of "The Man Who Couldn't Die." (See pages 40 and 73.) The author knew many of the men about whom he writes and the cases on which they worked.

## THE AUTHOR

Cecil (Nobby) Clark was 17 when he enlisted as a constable in the B.C. Provincial Police. He served for 35 years — more than one-third of the force's 92-year history — rising to the rank of Deputy Commissioner. In so doing he maintained a tradition of which the force was very proud — all senior officers, with the exception of the first appointment in 1858 when the force was born, rose from the ranks.

After Clark's retirement in 1950 his active service didn't end, it simply changed direction. Since the force had only about 100 members when he joined, he knew many of the pioneer policemen and worked on the later cases, interrogating rum-runners, thieves and murderers. He became the force's unofficial historian, but instead of writing a history which few people would read, Clark presented a popular cross-section of the force's hundreds of cases.

To complement his personal knowledge, he spent years researching in the Provincial Archives in Victoria, various libraries and official police records. The dry evidence he uncovered he transformed into tales of adventure and suspense that take the reader on a journey from the frontier British Columbia of the 1860s to the 1950s when the B.C. Provincial Police was absorbed by the Royal Canadian Mounted Police.

# CONTENTS

## AUTHOR'S FOREWORD

When the B.C. Provincial Police force was absorbed by the RCMP in 1950, it had the distinction of being not only the first police force in what is now Western Canada, but also Canada's oldest territorial force. When it was formed in 1858 there wasn't a mile of road on what is today the B.C. Mainland, the Prairie was a lawless region known as Rupert's Land, while Canada was the name given to a small corridor along the St. Lawrence River to the Great Lakes. When the provinces of Alberta and Saskatchewan were created in 1905, the B.C. Police force was already nearly 50 years old, and in 1912 when Ontario and Quebec attained their present boundaries it had been upholding the law for 54 years.

During the almost century-long era that the B.C. Provincial Police were the front line of law and order they were always few in number. Even by 1900 there were only 100 to police an area some 50 per cent larger than France. They nevertheless maintained the peace and well, in some cases to the cost of their lives.

The work of these pioneer policemen is the theme of the chapters which follow. They functioned in a land once described by Canada's famed humorist Stephen Leacock as "an empire in itself" — albeit a rugged empire amidst a sea of snowcapped peaks. Some have dubbed

Constable J. C. Devlin on a patrol in January 1934 to bring back a trapper's body from 200 miles away. In the bitter Peace River winter he and his companions were two weeks just reaching the trapper's cabin. The trek went into police records as "merely a routine case and investigation."

A B.C. Police guard of honor. Uniforms were introduced in 1924, greatly increasing pride among the officers and respect by the public. The force was particularly proud of the fact that apart from the first appointment of Chartres Brew in 1858, all commanding officers began as constables.

it the land of exaggeration. Extremes is perhaps the better word, considering that among its offshore islands tides can race up to 16 knots, in mountain passes wintertime snowfall can be 65 feet, and temperatures range from 109 °F in the shade to -72 °F.

All of which emphasizes that the province's pioneer policemen had many discomforting days in the saddle, on snowshoes along lonely bush trails, in canoes and riverboats, and on the wind-aroused waters of B.C.'s multi-thousand-mile coastline. There are many recorded instances of them bringing their prisoners by horse and canoe 1,000 miles to a courtroom, or battling hundreds of miles in winter's cold and snow during an investigation. The following story from *The Shoulder Strap*, the force's official magazine, is an example:

"On January 31, 1934, word was received from the Peace River district that a man named Zeb Croteau, an old trapper, had been found dead in his cabin some 200 miles away. Constable J. C. Devlin, on patrol in that district, was despatched to investigate the case, and bring the body back to civilization.

"In company with Fred Chase and Fred Hasler, well-known trappers who knew Croteau, together with a coroner, the group left Dawson Creek at noon for a long, tedious journey. They travelled 100 miles to Eswein's Ranch and were there joined by Ted Strand, another trapper. The party snowshoed to Callihason Creek, 50 miles up stream, and en route engaged Pete Calio, his toboggan, and team of five dogs, the only one in the district.

"They didn't arrive at Croteau's cabin until February 13, after two weeks of battling the elements of nature. They examined the body, and found that death was due to natural causes. An inquest was unnecessary. The party then made its way back to Dawson Creek with considerable difficulty.

"That is the story. Merely a routine case and investigation. But there was danger every day, danger ranging from being engulfed in a blizzard to breaking through the ice of a northern stream. Only one mistake could result in the patrol turning into another northern tragedy."

For decades horses were the main means of travel with weeks in the saddle not uncommon, although horses were often replaced by canoes and boats in summer, snowshoes and dog teams in winter. Other policemen were adept with tiller and mainsail as they patrolled B.C.'s 5,000-mile coastline. Then in the 1890s came launches with open naphtha engines which were gradually replaced by a fleet of diesel-powered cruisers. Finally arrived the air age and some officers piloted planes.

But even at the outbreak of World War Two in 1939, travel in Northern B.C. was arduous. In 1935, for instance, Constable R. Meek was posted to the new Detachment of McDame Creek in Northern B.C. He was three weeks getting there from Vancouver. On his return just over three years later he arrived "outside" in only five days. On the trip he travelled 650 miles by plane, 787 by train and 110 by car — 1,547 miles to get from one detachment to another. Constable Meek, like one-third of B.C.'s police force, later joined the fight against Hitler. He served in the RCAF and became one of many former policemen decorated for bravery.

Perhaps it is needless for me to note that these tales of law enforcement are as factually correct as years of research can make them. But as they span a century, changes in jurisdiction and rank may occasionally be puzzling. For clearer understanding a little background information is perhaps appropriate.

In 1858 the sudden influx of tens of thousands of gold seekers into the rocky canyons of the Fraser River transformed the fur-trading character of Britain's Pacific Coast colony into a copy of the 1849 stampede to California.

To organize a constabulary in the newly proclaimed colony, Britain's Colonial Secretary despatched 43-year-old Sub-Inspector Chartres Brew of the Royal Irish Constabulary. Immediately on Brew's arrival, Governor Douglas appointed him Chief Inspector of Police. The date was November 19, 1858, and the site of the swearing-in ceremony Fort Langley on the Fraser River just east of today's Vancouver. At the same ceremony the Colony of British Columbia was born.

Brew's handful of locally recruited policemen soon extended their activities to a new gold strike on Williams Creek in the Cariboo Country. Later they were on hand when a fresh bonanza was uncovered at Wild Horse Creek in the southeast corner of the colony. Thereafter, whenever a miner found gold, a policeman was soon at his elbow.

With law enforcement in such hands and even though in 1858 over 30,000 heavily armed miners from the U.S. stampeded to the Fraser River, there was remarkably little lawlessness — despite the fact that miners out-numbered policemen by over one thousand to one. Hubert Howe Bancroft, the Pacific Northwest's foremost historian, observed: "Never in the pacification and settlement of any section of America have there been so few disturbances, so few crimes against life and property."

Murders were committed, of course, but the culprits were usually apprehended . Then they were swiftly tried and, if found guilty, usually hanged. The first judge on the Mainland of B.C. (then called the Colony of British Columbia) was Matthew Baillie Begbie. He was selected because Sir Edward Bulwer Lytton, Colonial Secretary in London, wanted a young, athletic man who in Lytton's own words: "Must be a man who could, if necessary, truss a murderer up and hang him from the nearest tree."

While Begbie didn't hang anybody himself, he became the terror of evil doers, a legend who established a formidable reputation. As noted in Heritage House book, *Wagon Road North — Historical Photos from 1863 of the Cariboo Gold Rush:*

"He always carried his robes and wore them wherever he held court, whether it be a tent, store, saloon, or cabin. He was called a hanging judge, but he never hanged a man the jury didn't convict, and

When the B.C. Police force was formed in 1858 there wasn't a mile of road in what is today the B.C. Mainland. During their near century of service transportation methods changed from pack horses to stagecoaches, then to trains, gas-powered vehicles and boats, and from propeller-powered planes to jets.

The stagecoach was photographed at Yale in 1868, about to leave on a nearly 400-mile journey to Barkerville. Other photos show one of the specially equipped highway patrol cars placed in service in 1935, Police Motor Launch No. 8 at Prince Rupert after returning from a winter patrol, and Sergeant-pilot Noel A. Beaumont with the Force's first plane, a Beaver which began service in October 1949.

The lower photo shows an officer at the Force's radio-telegraph network. The B.C. Police established the first short wave, radio communication network in North America.

hanging was the only legal penalty for murder. His drumhead justice was the law that American miners could understand; his fearlessness won the respect of all. He was willing to fight with fists or with law-books, and never relented. At Clinton he once sentenced a man and later in his hotel room heard the fellow's companions plotting to shoot him. The judge listened for awhile, then emptied his chamber pot over them.

"One miner summed him up thus: 'Begbie was the biggest man [6' 5"], the smartest man, the best looking man, and the damndest man that ever came over the Cariboo Road'."

Begbie's letters, preserved in the Provincial Archives, also show that he was a strong advocate of the need for more policemen and better pay and living conditions for the few who were on duty. During the Cariboo gold rush in the early 1860s he wrote that "...there was not a magistrate nor a constable to be met within the long ride from Lillooet to the Cariboo — a journey which took a loaded mule train an average of from 28 to 35 days, and which even a light horseman could not expect to accomplish under eight or ten days."

Of the policeman's pay he was very critical, noting that the police were "called upon to perform most thankless duties involving great personal fatigue, exposure and responsibility.... The rates of pay are notoriously insufficient to provide a constable in the Cariboo with more than one meal a day ... without allowing anything for clothes (which I need not remark are extremely expensive and rapidly worn out), tobacco, an occasional stimulant or any of the other extras which a rough mountain life justifies and almost demands...."

Begbie was equally appalled at the accommodation — or lack of it — provided for the policemen. "At Williams Creek, he wrote, "a log house was built by Mr. Elwyn, which, being divided across the middle, gave accommodation for writing in the one half (a space of about 12 by 16 feet) and on the other half (of equal size, but possessing the inestimable luxury of a fireplace) Mr. Elwyn, his secretary, and three constables, had bunks piled upon each other, in which each man could spread his blankets separately. At Van Winkle, Mr. O'Reilly had not found the means of providing himself with any such luxury and the whole of the business of the district had to be conducted in a tent, which was the sole protection against the weather for him, and the books and records of the district. The climate in the Cariboo is at times exceedingly wet, as in all high mountainous regions, and it is not unusual to have torrents of rain for a week together almost without intermission. The tent ... I suppose withstands the weather no better than my own, and although it answers very well in tolerable weather or even for a few days of rain and where the camp is changed from time to time, I find that my tent becomes occasionally covered with mildew in the inside, while it is impossible to keep books, etc., dry, and all writing and recording is carried on at the greatest inconvenience. Besides the ground being constantly cold and damp, and there being no opportunity of approaching a fire without going out into the heavy rain, all cooking or drying any articles of apparel becomes extremely irksome. All officers having to remain for any length of time in that district ought to be provided at least with one room having a fireplace where they may at least be sure to meet a dry place to lie on, and the means of warming themselves and drying their clothes, keeping their books, etc., and placing a table so as to be able to write."

But despite the low pay and harsh conditions, the pioneer policemen performed well. As Begbie wrote:

"As regards the various magisterial and police matters throughout the Colony the public have every reason to be satisfied with the services rendered. Those services could not be rendered without a degree of exertion and personal hardship, which perhaps a bare sense of simple duty would not always require, and which certainly are not elicited by any extraordinary remuneration or immediate reward; and which can therefore only be attributed to an anxious desire in every officer to do his very utmost in his own department, to the sacrifice of his ease and comfort and very often of his health."

Despite the hardships and sacrifices, these policemen served the Colony of British Columbia and, after the Colony became part of Canada in 1871, the province of British Columbia for almost a century. The far ranging officers policed an area larger than Washington, Oregon and California combined. They saw not only the coming of the telegraph, the telephone and electric light but also were on duty when the four-horse stagecoach gave way to the train, the automobile and the airplane. They readily embraced anything new that would make them more efficient and were proud that their experiments enabled them to establish the first city-to-city short wave police radio communication system in North America.

Whether assisting victims of fire or flood, escorting fugitives from foreign countries, or merely performing the daily routine of urban duty, these British Columbia policemen did it with pride born of a sense of history. Many died in the performance of their duty, expecting nothing more than that they be remembered.

Finally, I might add that in assembling material for this book, though many of the latter-day stories come from personal first-hand knowledge, those stemming from an earlier period required a good deal of research in British Columbia's Archives. I would indeed be remiss, therefore, if I failed to acknowledge my deep sense of gratitude to the late Provincial Archivist Willard Ireland and the very capable Archives staff. I also wish to thank the original publisher of these articles, "The Islander" Sunday magazine of the Victoria *Daily Colonist*, for permission to reprint them.

To the B.C. Provincial Police — the living and the dead — the men who served British Columbia so well, this book is dedicated.

Cecil Clark
Victoria, B.C.

Constable Geoffrey H. Aston of the Penticton Detachment. He served with the 17th Lancers and Royal North-West Mounted Police before joining the B.C. force.

# Murder on Okanagan Lake

Shackled together in the sternwheeler's cabin
the prisoners were apparently secure. Unfortunately,
one hadn't been thoroughly searched.

About nine o'clock on the frosty night of March 16, 1912, the door of Chater and Taylor's General Store and Post Office at South Kelowna slowly opened to admit a customer. He was roughly dressed in heavy work trousers tucked into the tops of muddy, high-laced boots, a mackinaw that bore traces of hard wear, and a cloth cap pulled low over his eyes.

Among those in the store were part owner Fred Taylor and a boy

The sternwheeler *Okanagan*, scene of the deliberate murder.

Top: Walter Boyd, alias Walter Boy James.

named Roy Randall. All stared incredulously at the stranger, but not because of the way he was dressed. Around his face was draped a dirty handkerchief, in his right hand he gripped a menacing revolver.

"Stick up your hands!" he snapped. Slowly, Taylor and his customers obeyed.

"That's right. Keep 'em that way," came the ominous injunction. The bandit stepped to one side and quickly looked around. As his eyes momentarily left the store's occupants, young Randall bravely slipped out and fled down the road.

With a curse the gunman bounded after him. The night silence was shattered by the crashing report of the .44 as he fired at the boy's retreating figure.

Coolly re-entering the store, the robber made for the till. It was empty. "Come on," he barked, "you have got some money around here. Where is it?"

He caught sight of a small safe.

"Open that up," he commanded. Taylor complied. The bandit scooped up its meagre contents. Then with a final snarled threat he backed out of the door. Thus began the brief career of one of the most quick-witted and cold-blooded criminals ever to challenge the B.C. Police.

In the meantime, young Roy Randall had burst into the crowded barroom of the nearby Bellevue Hotel. It was the aftermath of a Saturday rugby game and some 30 or 40 football fans crowded the bar. At first the boy had a hard time making anyone understand what had happened. But after he attracted attention someone got hold of Constable John Tooth, veteran B.C. Police officer stationed in Kelowna. He flashed word to nearby Provincial Police Detachments then made a thorough search of the locality.

Although the search failed to find a trace of the gunman, he was identified as Walter Boyd, alias Walter Boy James. He was a 24-year-old laborer who had worked for a local company, reputed to be a crack shot with pistol or rifle.

At Penticton, 40 miles away, Provincial Constable Geoffrey Aston noted the bulletin about the Kelowna robbery and Boyd's description. He immediately passed the information on to Penticton's municipal Police Chief Mike Roche.

Two days later, the wanted man and a companion entered Penticton's B.C. Hotel about 11 p.m. and asked for a room. One of the proprietor's, Thomson, recognized James by the description circulated by the police.

"Sorry, we haven't got a room left," he said. Then he suggested, as if an afterthought: "There's a rooming house at the end of the block. Why don't you try there? If they're full, come back here and maybe I can think of something."

When the two left, Thomson slipped round to the police station. Constable Aston immediately contacted Chief Mike Roche and Constable Bill Pope and they headed for the B.C. Hotel.

They were in luck. James and his companion had returned and were sitting quietly in the lounge, their backs to the street door. Drawing their guns, Roche and Aston stepped into the lounge. Before the surprised strangers could move they were overpowered and handcuffed. James' companion, who gave his name as Frank Wilson, said he had nothing to do with the Kelowna holdup.

"We'll hold him for a while, anyway," said Aston. As he handcuffed the pair Chief Roche pulled a .44 revolver out of James' inside holster. Unfortunately, all three officers overlooked doing a thorough search of him.

To take the prisoners back to Kelowna meant a trip on the lake

Frank Wilson who witnessed the murder of Constable Aston.

Below: The rotunda of the B.C. Hotel in Penticton where Boyd and Wilson were arrested.

steamer *Okanagan*, which left Penticton northbound about 5:30 in the morning. About 1 a.m. the three police officers took their prisoners to the *Okanagan*.

Aston and his prisoners were assigned to cabin 34. After seeing Aston remove the handcuffs, then leg-iron his prisoners in an upper berth, Chief Roche and his assistant left the ship. Twice before daylight a patrolling municipal policeman passed the ferry and noted that all was in order in cabin 34.

At 5:30 the sternwheeler's engines commenced their rhythmic throb as she headed for her first stop at Peachland. As the vessel churned the chilly waters of Okanagan Lake, James was formulating a plan to escape. One thing that was going to help was a little .22 revolver in a tiny leather holster under his armpit. The policemen had overlooked it in their search.

By the light of the small lantern in the cabin, James could see the Constable's kit bag in one corner, his coat hanging on the door, and a water jug and glass. He quickly formed an escape plan, but its execution must wait until the ship stopped at Peachland.

An hour passed. As the vessel chugged along, Constable Aston sat on the settee smoking his pipe. The only sound in the cabin was the dull reverberation of the ship's engines.

James broke the silence. "Can I have a drink of water?" He raised himself on his elbow and looked over the edge of the bunk.

Aston rose. Turning his back on the prisoner he filled the glass. When he turned, glass in hand, he found himself looking into the small but deadly muzzle of a .22 revolver.

"Stick up your hands," came James' low level command.

If Aston was startled, he didn't show it. Contemptuously he eyed the man with the gun and said: "Which one?"

"Both," said James.

Glass in hand, Aston ignored the order. Slowly he moved toward the bunk, extending the water to the prisoner. As if hypnotized by the policeman's steady gaze, James stretched out his left hand. In slow motion the glass changed hands. All the time the two pairs of eyes never ceased their intent challenge. Each man waited for the move that would break the spell. Even as James slowly passed the glass to Wilson behind him in the bunk, his eyes never left Aston's face.

Wilson, inwardly quaking at the potentially deadly confrontation, took the glass of water with trembling hand.

Suddenly James realized that Aston was taking another slow step nearer. The tension was broken by a sharp click as James pulled the trigger. The gun misfired!

Truly the gods had tipped the scales in Aston's favor, almost as if in admiration of his courage. But as Geoff Aston courageously sprang at James he fired again. This time there was a report. The police officer, shot through the head, swung around and collapsed on the cabin floor with a deep groan.

James compelled his bunk mate to join him and the pair feverishly searched the unconscious police officer for the leg-iron keys. They couldn't find them. Then James turned to the kit bag. Slitting it open with Aston's pocket knife he found no keys but pocketed a .38 Smith & Wesson revolver and a handful of shells.

"Might come in handy," he remarked to his shackled companion.

They finally found the leg-iron keys in the pocket of the coat on the door. Quickly the leg irons were removed and the pair sat down to plan their next move.

"We'll be stopping at Peachland in a few minutes," said James hurriedly, "and nobody's heard a thing. Only one man saw us come on the boat. That was the night clerk. He should be off duty now, and having a sleep."

Wilson shuddered as he viewed the figure of Constable Aston on the floor, a thin stream of blood from his head wound staining the carpet.

"Come on, pull yourself together," snapped James. "We'll be miles away before anyone comes in here."

Two doors led into the stateroom, one from the lounge inside the ship, the other from the deck outside. As the boat nosed into the Peachland dock, James left the inside door bolted, while he and Wilson left by the deck entrance. Armed and free, they slipped up the gangplank in the frosty chill of the mid-March morning.

At Peachland, below, Boyd and Wilson left the sternwheeler
*Okanagan.* Above are her officers, with Captain Estabrooks
sitting in the center. On his right is Mate A. J. Macdonald,
first to enter the cabin and find the dying police officer.

As James had predicted, the night clerk was off duty, but the departure of the two men did not go unnoticed. Alf Watson, the ship's purser, saw them leave and wondered who they were.

When the *Okanagan* was a mile or so from Peachland, Watson was still trying to figure out who these two men were because he hadn't booked any passengers for Peachland. He was so interested that he went back to his cabin to check the passenger list. There was no one booked for Peachland. A persistent person, Watson hunted steward Spencer Stovell. He was conversing with one of the passengers who was voicing suspicions about cabin 34. "I think whoever is in there, is sick," she said. "I've heard the most unusual noises."

Watson and Stovell immediately reported to the mate, Alec McDonald. The three went to the cabin and knocked. Getting no answer, they entered by the deck door.

McDonald, in the lead, recoiled in horror as he saw the still figure of Aston in a pool of blood. Quickly the injured man was lifted into the lower bunk. As he was lifted, he opened his eyes and smiled.

When the steamer reached Gallatly about 8 a.m., Constable Tooth at Kelowna was advised of the shooting and lake side telephones quickly relayed the news of the shooting. Big Geoff Aston was known and liked throughout the district, and many residents expressed in unmistakable terms what should be the fate of the murderer.

When the sternwheeler docked at Kelowna, Dr. Austin Huycke accompanied the injured policeman to hospital. There it was found that the bullet was so deeply imbedded in his brain that an operation was impossible. "Only a miracle can save him," declared the doctor.

Chief Constable P. G. Routh of B.C. Police Headquarters at Vernon took charge of the manhunt. Soon squads of Special Constables were posted on every road and trail, while small boats patrolled the lake. In addition, Indians from the Westbank Reserve, noted for their tracking skill, joined the intensive search. Since the snow-covered hills offered scant shelter to the hunted men, two ranchers from Wilson's Landing, P. H. L. Seeley and R. D. Ramsay, felt that they would stay close to the lake side and the wagon road.

They had been told to watch for strangers, the reason they carried Winchesters as they walked along the road on the morning of the second day of the search. Rounding a bend, they stopped suddenly. Two men were approaching. Quietly the ranchers stepped behind a big rock, each working the lever of his Winchester.

Nearer and nearer trudged the strangers, the ranchers recognizing them as the fugitives. As they passed the rock, Seeley stepped out. "Throw up your hands," he commanded.

James whirled around, in his hand Aston's .38 revolver.

"Drop it!" snapped Seeley, sighting along the barrel.

The revolver dropped harmlessly to the road. Both men were searched. Then, hands behind their necks, they were soon at the steamer landing. Once again they stepped aboard the *Okanagan*, again as prisoners. This time there was no chance for escape — an enthusiastic deck crew lashed the pair to a mast.

The steamer reached Kelowna on Wednesday, March 20. Word of the arrest had spread and the dock was jammed with sightseers. Through the throng the prisoners were hustled to the police station. It was soon evident that Wilson hadn't been an accomplice in the Kelowna holdup. He had met James afterwards.

Wilson's eye-witness account of the shooting on the *Okanagan* was valuable to the Crown when James was charged. Constable Aston, meanwhile, lingered 10 days before dying on March 28. James faced the magistrate again. This time the charge was "wilful murder."

Pending James' trial, it became part of jail routine to search him daily since he quickly proved to have an uncanny knack for getting hold of escape material, even though he was always shackled with heavy leg irons. As a guard ran his hands up and down his clothing, James would taunt him: "You're getting hot now."

Eventually some minute piece of metal would be discovered; something James felt he could use. On the day that he was to be escorted to Vernon for trial, a guard noticed something suspicious with his leg-irons. Close inspection revealed that both shackles had been sawed through. A small portion of hacksaw blade was found in the instep of James' shoe, stuck there with adhesive tape.

While the killer never overlooked anything that might help him escape, neither did the police. He went to Vernon leg-ironed and handcuffed between two prisoners.

Before Chief Justice Gordon Hunter, James heard a jury say "Guilty." He was sentenced to hang at Kamloops on August 9, 1912.

In his last days his father came to see him from the U.S. "What do you want?" snapped James when he caught sight of the elderly figure in the jail office.

"I've just come to see you, son," said the old man.

"Well, I don't want to see you," said James, and turned away.

As the execution date drew near, James was still planning a way to escape. For weeks he collected pepper and filled a paper tube with it, gumming the edges with porridge.

The day before his execution, guard Simson entered his cell with a meal. With a quick movement, the murderer blew the contents of the tube into Simson's eyes. Half-blinded, he staggered but swung at James with his fist. Stunned by the blow, James reeled back. It was just time enough for Simson to slam the cell door. Had James got hold of the keys, he likely again would have escaped.

On the day of his hanging two others were also scheduled to die on the gallows. Three scaffolds had been erected in the jail-yard, but at the last minute only two were needed. One sentence had been commuted to life imprisonment. It wasn't James's.

As he shambled up to his platform he turned to Warden Vicars and remarked: "So this is what you've been busy with the last few days. Why you haven't even got it painted!"

A suddenly taut rope brought silence.

Contrary to legend, nobody ever swung from the
lonely pine. But there are bodies beneath it. Here
is the myth and the reality of

# Hangman's Tree at Lillooet

Known for years as the "Hangman's Tree," a gnarled and twisted old
sidehill pine still stands on the bench land above Lillooet on the west
bank of the Fraser River. Although the tree's grim connotation holds
interest for summer tourists, there is no factual basis to the story that
in the late 1850s and early 1860s desperadoes swung from its lower
limbs.

One reason is that there has never been a lynching in British
Columbia. Another is that famous gold-rush judge, Matthew Baillie
Begbie, would never have permitted such a makeshift disposal of the

condemned. The men he sentenced were all hanged legally on proper scaffolds.

There have been, however, perhaps five burials beneath the spreading branches of this venerable tree, both Indians and whites. One of the latter was William Armitage, hanged at Lillooet on a crisp, late November morning in 1863. Maybe it was because of the manner of Bill's demise that the tree acquired its legend.

This unfortunate's name was not really Armitage. For seven years he had been known as George Storm. It was only when his death was hours away that he revealed his identity to his friend, Bob Stephenson, who had hastened from Yale to deliver a letter to him.

In the silence of the little log lockup the condemned man read the

Lillooet in 1863 when William Armitage became the first man hanged in the community.

Judge Matthew Baillie Begbie, the Cariboo's famous judge who pronounced the death penalty.

letter. After pondering briefly he drew from his finger a gold ring engraved with the crest of one of Britain's oldest titled families. Handing it to Stephenson, he remarked in low tones: "I seem to have made a complete mess of my life. Take this and send it back to my father and tell him I died of a broken neck when I was thrown from my horse."

As Stephenson took the ring, Armitage went on to speak remorsefully of his wife. "Do whatever you can for her. She always admired you."

Bob Stephenson had much to think about as he rode the mountain trail out of Lillooet. He had seen the execution and watched the brief and simple burial. Now his thoughts went back seven years to the young couple, both in their late teens, with whom he left England. They were George Storm and his new bride. Both were much in love, both looking forward to life in the new world.

At New York, the Storms and Stephenson transferred to a ship to begin the long journey to San Francisco. When they arrived several weeks later they had a farewell dinner and separated. The Storms headed northward into the gold-rich country around Placerville, while Stephenson remained in San Francisco.

Stephenson heard nothing further of the Storms. In 1862 came word of a fabulous gold strike in the Cariboo region of British Columbia. Stephenson saw fortune beckon and headed north over 1,000 miles to the new goldfields. Like most of his fellow adventurers, he found little but disappointment. Finally, however, a claim he staked on Lightning Creek proved a bonanza. By late summer of 1863 he had sent some $50,000 to the Bank of British North America in Victoria. (Over $1.5 million at today's price of gold.)

Stephenson was unusual in that unlike most miners he guarded his hard-won treasure. He was a quiet, methodical man, perhaps the reason that he had little desire for Barkerville's saloons, preferring to spend his evenings in his hillside cabin.

Just before leaving Barkerville, however, he decided to visit the raucous community. Wending his way along the high plank sidewalk that fringed Barkerville's mud-holed main street, he stepped by chance into a saloon and dance hall. Here in the smoky reek of kerosene lamps, against a background of fiddles and mouth organs, the miners danced and drank their gold away.

In the noisy crowd, Stephenson glanced at one of the hurdy girls. Ostensibly employed to dance with the miners at a dollar a minute, their main job was to see that the mud-encrusted men from the creeks were steered to the bar as often as possible. Stephenson stared at the girl. Suddenly he realized she was George Storm's wife.

Startled, he began wondering how the charming bride of seven years ago had become a dancer in a honky-tonk bar. Eventually he steered her into an anteroom where she told him a story of disillusionment and frustration. It all began in California where her husband had began to gamble, a fever he couldn't shake.

For years, she told Stephenson, they had gone by different names, leading a nomadic existence in the American southwest. Finally as Bill

Hurdy-Gurdy dancers at Barkerville. For a dollar a minute they danced with the miners then steered them to the bar where their gold rapidly vanished.

The main street a few days before Barkerville burned to the ground in 1868.

and Bella Armitage, they had come to Barkerville. Bella worked the miners in saloons and dance halls while Bill "bucked the tiger" in some nearby faro game. When, more often than not, he was cleaned out, they lived on Bella's earnings.

For Stephenson the story was sordid and tragic. When he contacted Armitage the next day, he tried to get him to quit the gaming tables for Victoria and a respectful job. As they talked, however, he noticed that the once bright and carefree young Englishman was now hard and cynical, apparently feeling that he could earn money without having to work honestly.

A day or two later Stephenson noticed that Armitage had a close friend, a smooth and hard-eyed gambler called Fred Glennard. He was an American who by his looks had slipped out of California ahead of a vigilante committee.

Soon after that Stephenson left Barkerville for Yale on the Fraser River. That fall he was surprised to see Bella Armitage step from the stagecoach. On speaking to her, he noticed that she was not only tired from the long dusty journey but also in great mental distress. She then told a story of a domestic tragedy in which Bill Armitage was the central figure.

After he had left Barkerville, Stephenson learned, Armitage and Glennard also pulled out. But instead of taking the stagecoach, they had hiked down the Cariboo Road. One night when they stopped at Murphy's near 141-Mile House, they met two businessmen called

The 108 Mile House in 1868, typical of the Cariboo roadhouses. At the 141 Mile House Armitage and his companion plotted to rob Taylor and Clegg.

Taylor and Clegg. Clegg, the younger, had arrived on a horse; Taylor on a mule. Clegg had been making cash collections for a Victoria firm and had a considerable sum of money in his saddlebag, something Armitage and Glennard quickly noted.

Next morning Armitage and Glennard left early, but a few miles down the trail they waited in ambush. Along came Taylor and Clegg, but this time Clegg rode the mule and Taylor the horse. The change confused the highwaymen. They attacked and killed Clegg and fled with his worthless saddlebag.

The sudden exchange of gunshots startled Taylor's horse. It bolted down the trail carrying its rider and Clegg's well-filled saddlebag. Taylor quickly recovered control of his mount but when he returned all he found was Clegg's bullet-ridden body.

He rode to Mud Lake and reported to District Police Chief William G. Cox. An immediate search commenced. With the help of skillful Indian trackers the police eventually found the embers of the robbers campfire, beside it Clegg's empty saddlebags. Finally they found Glennard's body on a Thompson River sandbar where he had drowned trying to ford the swift-running river.

A day or two later Armitage was captured in the Bonaparte country, his only possessions a few raw potatoes and a pearl handled .44 Colt. A gunsmith in Lillooet later identified the weapon as Clegg's.

Committed for trial, Armitage appeared before Judge Begbie at a Lillooet Assize. Armitage's defence was that Taylor, bouncing in the saddle of his bucking horse, had fired at the robbers and killed Clegg by mistake. The jury rejected this plea and Begbie pronounced the death sentence.

Bella Armitage told Stephenson that the execution was only a week off, and she had a favor to ask. She had written a letter to her husband, the last he would ever read. Would Stephenson take it to Lillooet before the executioner did his duty?

A week later Bob Stephenson visited Armitage in his final moments. When he was handed the family ring, only then did Stephenson learn the true identity of William Armitage. He was a baronet's younger son who, on impulse, had eloped with one of the family's maids. It was only after their arrival in California that the two were legally married.

After the execution, Stephenson returned to Yale. Not long after Bella Armitage left B.C. for California. A few months later Stephenson followed. A year later a Victoria resident noticed a brief news item in the *San Francisco Bulletin*. Mrs. Armitage had become Mrs. Stephenson.

The only link to the frontier tragedy is the gnarled old pine on a bench land behind Lillooet. This summer, as they have for years, tourists will trudge up the hill to photograph it. There's nothing, of course, to photograph — the story is under their feet!

The remains of Forster's magnificent ranch home.

# Death Rode a Pinto Pony

"Murder, though it have no tongue, will speak with most miraculous organ," wrote William Shakespeare. In East Kootenay some 400 years later a pinto pony and a broken water pipe spoke eloquently of murder in the peaceful Windermere Valley.

In the Windermere Valley in southeastern B.C. the 1940 autumn had turned the trees to red and gold, sending the last tourists homeward. The bustle of summer over, residents prepared for the "quiet time" of winter. Their anticipated tranquility, however, was shattered by a brutal double murder in their Valley.

The first suggestion of trouble seemed innocent. Justice of the Peace Frank Richardson in the community of Athalmer learned that a house had been destroyed by fire. From the general location, Richardson felt that it must be Ernie Forster's place near Brisco. It was curious, he thought, that Ernie himself hadn't reported his loss.

Richardson phoned B.C. Police Constable Jack White in neighboring Invermere to see what he knew. It was news to White. But if the story were true, he was interested. Under the Fire Marshall's Act there were forms to fill out stating how the fire started, what companies held the insurance and so forth. Late that afternoon Constable White and local Game Warden Alec Sinclair started out for the house.

As he drove, White thought about Ernie Forster, a 72-year-old recluse who lived in lonely splendor in a 10-room mansion built many years ago when he was comparatively wealthy. The house was seven miles north of Wilmer on a route to Brisco that old-timers had dubbed "Horse Thief Road." Forster, a district resident for close to 40 years and a one-time member of the B.C. Legislature, had equipped the rambling colonial-style house with an automatic water supply and its own electric light plant. He had a family, but had lived apart from them for years.

It was dusk when the patrol car's headlights swung into the driveway of the Forster place. As the two officers got out, one thing was immediately obvious — the Forster mansion was the scene of the fire. Only three gaunt chimneys stood over a mass of blackened and charred debris that half filled the concrete basement.

There was no evident sign of life. Then White noticed that the garage was empty. Flashlight in hand, he and Sinclair walked around the ruins.

"Something funny down there," said White with sudden interest as he shot his light between the charred beams. Closer examination showed the objects to be bones — human bones! The pair decided to return at daylight and conduct a proper examination. With no near neighbors, nothing would be disturbed overnight.

At Invermere, White gave routine notice of the occurrence to his Cranbrook district senior Sergeant Harry Wood. He responded quickly, arriving in Invermere in time to accompany White, Sinclair and Coroner A.M. Chisholm to the Forster fire.

The fragments of bones proved to be human. Careful probing uncovered two rifles and a shotgun, as well as two revolvers and a watch. Then they made another gruesome discovery — the torso of a second man, face down, his arms, legs and head burned away. By a stroke of fate a broken water pipe had continued to spray on his back, saving the body from total destruction.

At a hastily summoned coroner's inquiry at Invermere, Dr. Coy identified the remains as those of Ernie Forster. The doctor was familiar with Forster since he had treated him for a spinal ailment. One other thing the inquest produced: a bullet taken from the dead man's body, a bullet that had killed him before the fire started!

Sergeant Wood and Constable White began to re-construct Forster's immediate past, hour by hour until his many-roomed house was consumed by roaring flames. They learned that nearby rancher Anton Raunch and his wife had noticed an unfamiliar Indian riding by on a pinto pony about a week before. The rancher thought that the pony might have belonged to an Indian called Eugene.

When the policemen investigated this new lead they learned that the horse belonged to Eugene Joe. He said he'd lent his pinto to another Indian, Frank Sylvester, two weeks before. The horse had come home to the barn without the rider, and Eugene hadn't seen Sylvester since.

Since Forster didn't travel much, neighboring settlers were unable to offer information about his movements. The liquor vendor at Invermere, however, revealed something interesting.

Forster had been in about September 25, bought two bottles of Australian wine and a dozen beer. With him was a man in his eighties called John Lundy. From their conversation, it seemed that Lundy was staying with Forster. They were buying the wine and beer because the elderly men had met two soldiers they wanted to treat. The soldiers had a car and were all going to Forster's for supper.

Records showed that an older model Chevrolet was registered in Forster's name. A police pick-up order for the car was flashed around South Kootenay police posts. Then Sergeant Wood phoned Constable F. L. Jeeves at the Cranbrook office and asked if he knew Frank Sylvester. Yes, Jeeves knew him.

"Get hold of him and check his movements around the latter part of September," was the order.

Jeeves didn't bother to add that his knowledge of Sylvester had occurred only the night before. He had been having a late meal in the deserted White Spot restaurant when an Indian walked in. After one look at the lone customer in khaki and green, he turned and walked out.

"Got a guilty conscience," thought Jeeves. Dropping his knife and fork, he hastened after the man and asked him his name.

Frank Sylvester was the reply, and he lived on St. Mary's Reserve nearby.

"Better get back there," advised Jeeves, and returned to his meal.

Now he was under orders to find the Indian. As he walked through the outer office he noticed a prisoner's property spread out on a table.

"Pity these fellows couldn't put this stuff in property bags instead of leaving it lying around," he thought as he idly picked up a driver's licence. To his astonishment, Frank Sylvester's name was on it.

Jeeves learned that Constable Bob Ring had just brought him in, drunk. He'd been annoying people on the street. Jeeves advised Sergeant Wood that the search for Sylvester had been completed in under 30 seconds. The only problem was that he'd have to wait until Sylvester sobered up.

Then news of the missing blue Chevrolet came from a Greyhound bus driver. He had been stopped on the highway between Banff and Cranbrook about 4 a.m. one day in late September to help two Indians stalled in an old blue Chev. One of the men answered the description of Frank Sylvester. Only a day or so before he had flagged the bus near Invermere and bought a ticket to Cranbrook. Next night he'd been checked on the street by Jeeves, and the following morning picked up drunk by Ring.

While the mystery man, Sylvester, remained behind bars nursing his throbbing head, Jeeves decided to search the trails and by-ways for some sign of the missing car. By a coincidence, passing through Cranbrook that morning was Corporal J. Locke, departmental transport expert on a routine check of police equipment.

"Come along for the ride," suggested Jeeves. Hour after hour the pair drove, then in a patch of brush off a trail at Ta Ta Creek they found an abandoned car. Nearby, under a log, was a Savage .30-30 rifle. The

car was out of gas, and missing from the steering column was the registration slip.

It was, nevertheless, an important clue. Then Sylvester's brother, Pierre, was found near Invermere. His information was to solve the case.

According to him, Frank had appeared one afternoon in an old blue Chev. He was pretty drunk and boastful, and took Pierre and his father for a ride. They got a bottle of beer each from Frank, but were a little suspicious of his new-found wealth. When he said goodbye and drove off it was with the intention of meeting Willie Stephens and giving him a drink, Pierre said.

"Willie Stephens?" said White to Sergeant Wood. "I know him."

Found on the reserve, Willie told his story in the Invermere police office. It was a story that came in halting syllables, a story of cold-blooded murder and arson that shocked Valley dwellers.

It was about September 28, Willie related, when Frank Sylvester came to his shack about midnight. He had something to tell, something important. He wouldn't go into the shack; he'd tell it out in the open.

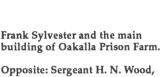

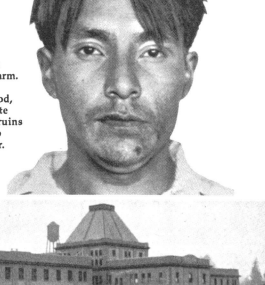

Frank Sylvester and the main building of Oakalla Prison Farm.

Opposite: Sergeant H. N. Wood, far left, and Constable J. White discovered the bodies in the ruins and led the investigation into what proved a double murder.

Making sure he was far enough away from any dwelling, he told Willie he'd killed two men.

More boasting, thought Stephens, and asked who the men were.

"Forster," said Sylvester, "and another old man who lives with him."

"I don't believe it," scoffed Stephens.

"Come with me, I'll show," Sylvester challenged.

The pair walked the 10 miles to Forster's. It was a moonlit night as they approached Forster's house. Although the mansion was in darkness, Sylvester unhesitatingly climbed the front steps between the tall colonial pillars. Instead of knocking, he turned the handle and walked in. Willie didn't like any part of events and was all for leaving. Sylvester, however, grabbed him by the arm and pulled him into the hallway, then snapped on a light.

Through the dimly lit hall the pair went, Sylvester leading. There was a huge living room off to one side. Sitting by an immense fireplace was the room's sole occupant — Jim Lundy. He appeared to be asleep in the big comfortable chair, his chin on his chest. But a shaft of moonlight through a nearby window spotlighted the elderly figure, show-

31

ing a blackened patch of dried blood on one side of his white head. He was dead, shot through the head.

"Let's get out of here!" was Willie Stephen's hoarse reaction. But Sylvester told him to shut up.

"There's a bottle around here somewhere if we can find it," was Sylvester's main concern as he rummaged through a sideboard.

Stephens had a hard time keeping his eyes off the man in the chair. Then something else rivetted his attention. Sylvester had gone up the wide stairway to the upper floor in his search for liquor, stepping over something on the way.

To Willie's added terror and horror he saw it was the body of another man, lying face down near the top of the stairs.

Successful in finding the remains of a bottle of wine, Sylvester next crumpled old newspapers. A quick trip to the kitchen and he returned with a can of kerosene and splashed the contents along the woodwork by the papers. Then he struck a match. In seconds tongues of flame were licking up the walls.

The two Indians fled and ran for half a mile. At first there was smoke, said Willie, but later when they looked back, "Big flame. House all on fire."

Sylvester had threatened him with death if he ever spoke of the night's work, and he hadn't seen Sylvester since.

"Did he tell you how the men got killed?" inquired Constable White.

Willie nodded. Sylvester said that a week before the house was burned he was looking for liquor, and he thought he might get old Forster to give him a drink. Riding up on a borrowed pinto pony to a patch of brush that screened the house, he threw the reins over a low hanging branch and peered through the bushes. There was a car outside. Approaching stealthily, Sylvester saw through a window the two elderly men sitting having a drink with two soldiers. He watched until the soldiers left, then shot Lundy through one of the windows as the old man sat in his chair. Forster rushed into the room at the sound of the shot. As he looked toward the window, Sylvester fired again.

Hit in the shoulder, Forster made a dive for the stairs, probably to get a rifle from the gun rack on the landing. But he died near the top of the stairs.

Then, Sylvester told Stephens, he entered the house and picked up a bottle of wine and four bottles of beer. When he came out into the garden he found his horse gone. It had been startled by the shots and made off. So he took Forster's car out of the garage and drove away.

"What kind of rifle did Frank have?" queried White, thinking of the Savage carbine found near the abandoned car at Ta Ta Creek.

"A Savage rifle," said Willie, "a .30-30."

One more point Willie added. Sylvester had taken the registration slip off the steering column of Forster's car, tore it in bits and threw it out the car window.

"Where?" asked White.

"Oh, I dunno. Somewhere along the road," he said.

Constable Jeeves found the scraps of paper, every one of them. They were important corroboration.

Sylvester, meantime, was spending a week of his drunk penalty in the Cranbrook cells, unaware of the busy investigation around him. One morning, however, he decided he wanted to make a statement. He related how he'd waited till the soldiers left the Forster place, then begged a drink from Forster. He wanted another, but couldn't get it. Then he wanted to buy a bottle, and Forster grabbed a gun and told him to get off the premises.

"I'll tell the police you sold me liquor," Sylvester yelled by way of a threat, and Forster fired at him. Sylvester shot him, then turned to see Lundy with a gun, and shot him.

It was a weak alibi because he'd told Willie Stephens that he had shot Lundy through the window as he sat in his chair. The police picked up proof of this admission in two empty cartridges near a flowerbed in front of what had been a window. Furthermore, Willie Stephens had seen Lundy dead in the chair.

The bullet taken from Forster's body and Sylvester's rifle were handed to ballistics expert Detective-Sergeant J. Young who had arrived to help in the investigation. As Young studied the slightly misshapen slug, Sergeant Wood asked him, "What equipment do you need to make a comparison with the .30-30 rifle?"

"A comparison microscope and a camera to take microphotographs. Got them handy?" was Young's challenging reply.

There was need for speed, for Sylvester would come up for his preliminary hearing in two days. The bullet and gun would be a clinching piece of evidence. Unfortunately, the nearest equipment was in Victoria. There was, however, an RCMP crime lab in Regina. Although Regina was about the same distance away as Victoria, the latter route entailed a ferry which could take up to seven hours. A phone call to Regina assured the B.C. Police Officers of swift co-operation. Even though it would be Thanksgiving Day when they arrived, the lab would be open, its personnel waiting.

Young and Wood set off with the rifle and bullet. With only stops for food and fuel they reached the Regina lab in a record-breaking 14 hours over the gravel roads. The tests told the B.C. men what they wanted to know. Sylvester's gun had fired the fatal shot. With hastily dried micro-photographs in their briefcase, the two men hurried back to Cranbrook in time to give their evidence.

Committed for trial, Frank Sylvester came up before Mr. Justice A. M. Manson at the Fall Assize. A 12-man jury listened to the Crown put together the pieces of evidence. To them there was no doubt about Sylvester's guilt.

As a consequence, the man who rode a pinto pony down Horse Thief Road found himself four months later walking down Murderer's Row at Oakalla to meet the hangman.

The unusual open air courtroom at the site of the murder. From left are Constable J. J. McConnell, seated in the peaked cap is accused Charlie Roy, the standing woman is Mrs. Eocene Paul, while the man seated facing the two pairs of boots is Chief Justice Gordon Hunter.

Bottom left: Kamloops in the early 1900s. The murder took place on a flat reached by the bridge in the left of the photo.

The murder not only netted the killer less than $50 but also resulted in a trail of

# Footprints to the Gallows

This case started on January 3, 1915, on the bench land at the foot of Paul Mountain across the river from Kamloops. Here Basil Paul had a wood-floored tent which he and his wife, Eocene, occupied every summer when they came to put in a potato crop near Scheidam Creek.

On this winter afternoon Basil's wife had gone to the tent with their eight-year-old son for poplar bark to make traditional Indian cough medicine. She was surprised to see smoke coming from the tent's chimney. On investigating she found two roughly dressed men — one standing in the tent, the other lying on the bed.

"We're just travelling through," said one. "We got a little tired and needed some sleep. Be gone tomorrow."

Eocene nodded, collected her bark and returned home. When Basil learned about the two men, he left next morning to investigate. When he pulled the tent flap aside he got a shock. Only one man was there. He was lying in a welter of blood — and was very dead.

Basil reported his find to the Provincial Police in Kamloops and quickly a party headed by Inspector W. L. Fernie was on its way. The group included Constables Fiske, Gammond and Dallin, along with Dr. Burris and two Indian trackers, Charlie and Phillip Thomas.

When they arrived at the fence gate, 150 feet from the tent, Fernie briefed them in his usual methodical manner. In order not to confuse the tracks in the snow, Basil would first take his wife to the tent and identify the dead man. When they returned, Eocene reported that the man on the cot was clean shaven, whereas his companion had a moustache.

After questioning by Inspector Fernie, she added that the missing man was about 30, thin faced with black hair, wearing dark work pants, a mackinaw, cap with ear flaps and heavy work boots. He spoke, she thought, with a trace of a foreign accent.

With these details in his notebook, Constable Fiske returned to

Kamloops where he alerted the City and CPR Police. The town was combed for the fugitive but it was apparent he wasn't there. Fiske despatched telegrams giving the wanted man's description.

Meanwhile, at the tent the two Indian trackers had started to explore the area. In 15 minutes they rejoined the group at the gate with an amazing report. They said two men had slept in the tent Saturday night. One wore work boots minus both heels; the other, boots which lacked the left heel. The boots without heels were beside the dead man. On two occasions the previous morning, "One heel" had rustled wood for the stove but having no axe had been forced to pick up dead twigs. Along with the sticks he had picked up some dead sunflower stems. Two stems had fallen by the stove, thus giving a clue to where the wood had been collected.

The trackers hadn't been told about Eocene's visit the previous

Constable William Fernie, at far left, and one of his Indian trackers, Phillip Thomas, last man on the right. This photo was taken after Fernie and his trackers played a major role in capturing train robber Bill Miner. (See Heritage House book, *Bill Miner . . . STAGECOACH AND TRAIN ROBBER.*)

37

day. However, they reported that a woman had come in a buggy, gone to a tree to cut bark, and then over to the tent where she stood at the entrance.

"Small child come running from buggy near fence," concluded Charlie Thomas, "and stand beside woman at tent. Then she picked up bark and both go to buggy."

Although Eocene had not mentioned the boy running up to her, to the Thomas brothers it was as clear as reading a book. Their astute observations were incredible, especially considering the varied weather that had occurred in the 24 hours since Eocene had first seen the two men.

It had turned mild by Sunday morning, so mild that rain fell. Then, as reported by the Kamloops weather office, toward midday the temperature dipped to freezing, the rain turned to snow and by nightfall was 27°F. On Monday, when Basil arrived at the tent, the temperature was even lower, a condition that meant the trackers had to reconcile the footprints with time and weather.

Continuing their story, the trackers said that both men had left the tent "after it snowed a bit" (Sunday afternoon), gone toward the Thompson River Bridge, then returned to the tent.

Later, "One heel" had come out of the tent and picked up something that had become covered with fresh snow (proving he knew its location on Saturday), then gone into the tent and come out again. Later, Charlie Thomas pointed to the place where the "something" had lain.

The object was about 2 feet long and 3 inches thick. Whatever it was, it wasn't now in evidence. On the chance that it had been thrown away, however, Constable Gammond studied an ice-covered ditch until he noticed where the surface had recently been broken and refrozen. Baring his arm, he brought up from beneath the ice the coulter from a plow — a 6-pound piece of metal that matched the indentation near the tent. Unfortunately, it had been washed clean.

While the two trackers checked footprints along the wagon road toward the Thompson River Bridge, Fernie and Dr. Burris examined the corpse. He was about 25 and had died of two skull fractures some five to ten hours earlier. Although hands and feet were cold, the torso was still warm, some of the blood still wet. Against this condition the police had to consider that though the dead man was warmly clad, the temperature had dropped to 7 degrees of frost.

Next to his skin was an empty money belt. In one pocket was a small black book printed in Russian with the name "Michael Syrnyk" on the fly leaf. The book contained two pieces of paper, each bearing a mark similar to the ace of clubs. One was numbered 2423; the other, 2424.

The tent was empty except for a stove, a spring cot without a mattress and a headless axe handle that bore no marks of violence. Fernie took measurements and noted blood splashes on the tent wall near the head of the cot. He felt that because the man's head rested on his rolled up mackinaw, he had been murdered in his sleep.

While Fernie and Burris were busy with their examination, Constable Dallin took plaster casts of the footprints in the snow. It was a tricky job, the water inclined to freeze as it was dribbled on the plaster of paris. Despite the primitive conditions, he got good prints which even showed the nails in the soles.

As he finished this task, the Thomas brothers came back with a further report. They had traced "No heels" and "One heel" to the bridge where the tracks mingled with others. However, they picked up tracks showing that the pair had returned from Kamloops Sunday afternoon.

On the way back they had walked apart, one on each side of the road. Once "One heel" stopped to pick up something, perhaps left on their way into town. By the impression in the snow they felt it was a bedroll. Their assessment was later proved correct.

The quick eyes of the trackers noted where the two had stood talking. Here "One heel" had lit a hand rolled cigarette, a deduction based on their finding a burnt match and cigarette butt.

Meantime, among those who got Fiske's telegraphic description was Constable J. J. McConnell at the nearby Chase Detachment. He read it with the knowledge that no eastbound freight or passenger train had come through from Kamloops that day. At that moment, however, a westbound freight pulled in. He climbed into the cab and as they headed westward he and the engineer scanned both sides of the track.

McConnell found nothing at Shuswap, then luckily grabbed another freight that took him to Monte Creek. In the waiting room was his man. He said his name was Charles Roy, and he had $41.80 in his pockets. That night Roy lodged in Kamloops jail. Inspector Fernie took possession of his shoes because the left one had no heel. Next morning Eocene Paul identified him in a line-up of six roughly dressed men taken at random from the streets.

The numbered slips found on the dead man proved interesting. They had been issued by a Kamloops labor agency to the murdered Mike Syrnyk, and were good for two trips to and from a CNR tunnel construction camp at Mile 127 on the North Thompson River.

Syrnyk had received a pay cheque when he left, and his travelling companion was Charles Roy. Inspector Fernie linked this news with the footprints from the tent to town. The police found the restaurant where Syrnyk cashed his cheque on Sunday afternoon — and Roy was with him. He had undoubtedly murdered the unfortunate Syrnyk for less than $50.

During the trial five months later, the entire court went to see the tent, and that is when the photograph used at the beginning of this story was taken. The jury said "guilty." Then fate and Chief Justice Hunter picked a proverbially unlucky date for the last chapter of Charlie Roy's life.

In 1915 he was hanged at Kamloops — on Friday, August 13.

# On the Trail of the Canton Giant

**The brutal murder of Richmond's one-man police force threatened to erupt into B.C.'s first lynching.**

There are few big men among southern Chinese, the men of Canton who have made up the bulk of our Oriental population. Yip Luck was one of the exceptions, a husky six-footer. In addition to his distinctive size, he was also to unknowingly have two other distinctions, both resulting from the fact he was on trial for murder. At a gesture from court interpreter Charlie Cumyow, he rose in the prisoner's box at the Vancouver Fall Assize one morning in early October, 1900.

On the bench sat Mr. Justice Paulus A. Irving. Below him at a desk was the Crown counsel, short and stocky W. J. "Bill" Bowser — slated one day to be B.C.'s premier. When the interpreter translated the charge the prisoner gave him a baleful look and muttered a brief reply.

"He says he pleads guilty," Cumyow told the court.

"Does he thoroughly understand what he's doing?" was the Judge's question.

"Yes, he quite understands," said Cumyow.

"Has the prisoner any counsel?" pursued the Judge.

"No, my lord," replied Bill Bowser.

"And now what do I do?" ruminated his lordship.

Steveston in the early 1900s.

"You can accept his plea, my lord," was Bowser's quiet comment.

The judge made a brief entry in his bench book that read: R(egina) v. Yip Luck — pleads "Guilty."

After that Yip was taken back to jail. Without any evidence being heard, Yip would appear again at the end of the Assize for sentencing.

The background to this slightly offbeat legal drama started six months earlier on Saturday, April 14, in the little fishing community of Steveston in Richmond, near Vancouver. It had a population of 350 and a one-man police force — Alexander Main. He was a 35-year-old Scot who for three years had been the "Chief of Police" of Steveston. Quietly authoritative, he commanded deep respect from fishermen — drunk or sober — for the firm manner in which he handled the Saturday night brawlers. To the public he was Alec; to his wife, Sandy.

The Mains, a childless couple, had breakfast about 7:30 Saturday morning. Around 8:00 Alec left, his Newfoundland dog with him. He said that he didn't know if he would be home for lunch. Apart from a few dollars in his pocket, the only other items he carried were the old-fashioned Beans handcuffs in his hip pocket, his badge and a notebook and pencil. Because municipal funds were insufficient to provide a uniform, he was dressed in his second-best blue suit. About 10 a.m. someone noticed him talking to a Chinese on Steveston's main street. Another seemed to recollect he'd seen Main walking along the dike east of town. From then on he disappeared — simply vanished among the dikes and marshland of Lulu Island.

Late that night, when he did not return home, his wife went to bed but not to sleep. Every hour she expected to hear his footsteps outside the cottage door. While she well knew that a rural policeman's hours were often irregular, at daybreak she began to worry. She went to the village to make enquiries. Among her other concerns was that Alec had suffered a heart attack since he'd been complaining about a pain in his chest.

None of the people she woke that Sunday morning had seen her husband. Next she asked Willett Steves and his two brothers who ran the Steveston to Vancouver horse stage. They couldn't help. The sympathetic Steves boys, however, organized a search for the missing man. By evening, weary from scanning sloughs and dikes, the searchers had nothing to report.

Sunday night passed still without sign of the policeman. Early Monday morning almost the whole township turned out to search. Volunteers probed and quested but by nightfall there was not a clue. Fishermen searching up and down the river also reported no sign of Alec Main.

Word of Main's disappearance eventually reached Vancouver Police Chief John M. Stewart who put a bulletin on the notice board. One of his men, Detective Thomas H. Wylie, was a friend of the Mains. After reading the bulletin he received time off to help search for his friend.

Early on Tuesday morning Wylie arrived in Steveston. He quickly learned that the only clue was the suggestion that someone had seen Main talking to a Chinese. Pursuing this lead, he phoned Lee Koy, president of Vancouver's Amalgamated Chinese Benevolent Societies. Often in the past, Lee had been of help to Wylie in cases involving Chinese. Again he wanted Lee's help.

Two hours later Lee Koy joined Wylie in Steveston. Then they methodically explored the shacks and sheds in Steveston's Chinatown. By midday they had found their man. He was Wo Lee, a market gardener who had spoken with Main on Saturday morning about the whereabouts of another Chinese, Yip Luck. Wo Lee told Main that Yip lived with two other men in a cabin near the dike about a mile east of town.

It was the first genuine lead. Wylie decided to follow it, picking out four townsmen to help him, including blacksmith George Shea who owned a bloodhound. By mid-afternoon the five and Lee Koy walked along the dike east of Steveston until they reached a clearing where Yip Luck's cabin stood. It was a clapboard, one-room unpainted structure with a lean-to shed at the rear. Nearby was a chicken run and a roofed-over pit for root vegetables.

Wylie pushed open the cabin door and in the gloom confronted two Chinese. One was a big man, powerfully built, with a forbidding look. They gave their names as Yip Luck and Chung Chee-Chong. It was evident that Chee-Chong, bothered by an incessant cough, was far from healthy.

Questioned through interpreter Lee Koy, the two men said they hadn't seen anything of Main. Veteran policeman Wylie, however, instinctively felt that there was something suspicious about their manner. As Lee Koy kept them in conversation, Wylie checked the cabin.

In a corner he picked up a pair of overalls — the seven-pocket style usually worn by railroad men, never bought by Chinese. There was something in one of the pockets. Wylie pulled out a pipe case. Inside on a chamois leather lining was an expensive Meerschaum pipe. It was not the kind usually smoked by Chinese, who preferred their water pipe. Questioning Luck and Chee-Chong about the overalls and pipe, Wylie received only sullen looks.

The searchers then spread out around the building. Murchison, attracted by the potato pit, saw a handle sticking out of the potatoes. It was a steel-bladed, slightly curved brush hook. "Look at this," he said to Wylie, as he pointed to some dried brown stains on the handle.

"Looks like blood," said Wylie, noting the blade had recently been cleaned. Then he turned to Shea: "See if that dog of yours can pick up any scent from this handle."

Shea led the bloodhound to the brush hook. Nose to the ground, the dog circled then headed about 50 feet to where the ground had recently been turned. Shea picked up a stick and started to probe. Suddenly his stick met resistance. On his knees, Wylie moved the earth with his hands. Finally he uncovered some cloth. It was an ominous find.

With a shovel Wylie carefully dug until it was clear that the hole in the ground held the body of Richmond's one-man police force. Cause of death were wounds that defied description. Even Wylie, experienced and hardened to brutality, paled at the sight of his friend's body as it was lifted from its grave. Beneath the policeman was the remains of his dog.

Wylie then returned to the cabin. Through interpreter Koy he confronted the Chinese with the gruesome discovery. Yip Luck denied any knowledge of the killing, but Chung Chee-Chong pointed at his companion and shouted in Cantonese: "He killed him — he killed him with the axe!"

Promptly the pair were searched, handcuffed together and taken to Steveston. Wylie took charge of the overalls and the pipe in case they were related to the policeman's murder. Of Main's handcuffs and badge there was no trace. His notebook which might have held a clue to his last enquiries was also missing. None was ever recovered.

Dr. R. B. McKibbon reported that Main had been killed by a blow from a sharp instrument which had cut deep into his head. The unfortunate man appeared to have seen the blow coming for there was another cut in his left forearm above the wrist. Probably after death his throat had been cut by some sharp instrument, a gash that had gone through to the vertebrae. Then, added the doctor, possibly the same sharp instrument had been used to hack the tendons behind Main's knees.

Coroner McGuigan conducted an immediate inquest and the result was a murder verdict. Late that evening as Yip Luck and Chung Chee-Chong paced their wooden cells in the police station, there was a tense atmosphere around Steveston. Grim-faced townsmen and fishermen clustered, a purpose to their action. Veteran policeman Wylie sensed that their mood could easily result in B.C.'s first lynching.

He immediately phoned the B.C. Provincial Police. By 10:00 p.m., as a large crowd collected around the lockup, Provincial Constable Colin S. Campbell drove up in a buggy. Wordlessly, he pushed through the crowd. Minutes later he reappeared with the two handcuffed Chinese. Silently the mob opened up. Campbell, pushing his charges before him, climbed into the rig and left for the safety of the New Westminster provincial jail.

Here Chung Chee-Chong, now completely unnerved, confessed that a third man had been involved in the crime. He was Ah Wong, a recent arrival from China who spoke no English. Apparently, he had fled the murder scene on Sunday morning.

When Wylie heard about the third man, he again began searching Lulu Island with Lee Koy. A check of rowboats and small craft near the wharves showed that none was missing, so the fugitive was still on the island. One thing was sure — he hadn't gone to Vancouver by stage. To make escape more difficult Wylie cautioned the local telephone operator to monitor all outgoing calls made by Chinese. "Whenever they start talking," was his injunction, "cut them off right away."

Then Wylie left to attend Alec Main's huge funeral in Vancouver, with Vancouver City Policemen as pallbearers. Immediately afterwards, Wylie continued the search for Ah Wong. A day later he got a lead. A rowboat was reported missing. He called Ladner to alert residents and Blaine to warn U.S. immigration officials.

After that he hired a boat to Ladner. Meanwhile, Lee Koy had asked a Chinese friend to meet Wylie on the dock and the pair quickly began their search. Ah Wong, readily recognizable because of his slight build, had been there all right. He was last seen heading for the Semiahmoo Trail, the route to the border. Later that afternoon Wylie finally caught him and brought him back to Steveston.

Ah Wong proved to be an inoffensive man who gave his version of the Main case through an interpreter. He said it was about midday that Main arrived at the cabin, when only he and Chee-Chong were present. Main didn't say very much, but Wong gleaned from his companion that the policeman was searching for some tools stolen from local farmer Jim Whiteside. Yip Luck had stolen the stuff and the tools — a brace and bits, hammer and two saws — were scattered around the shed.

The overalls belonged to Whiteside and so did the pipe. As Main was examining the overalls, Yip loomed in the doorway, in his hand the brush hook. He stole up behind the policeman. He was about to bring his upraised weapon into action when Main half turned and tried to ward off the blow. Struck on the head, Main fell to the floor. Then Yip dealt him the second deadly blow across the throat.

The three men conferred — the ailing Chee-Chong who was in the final stages of tuberculosis and the frightened Ah Wong both feeling they were being involved in a crime in which they had had no part. They all went for a walk. On their return Yip grabbed a chicken from the hen run, cut off its head and cooked it. The three ate the chicken — the corpse on the floor as a witness. As Yip Luck explained, this would ward off any curse that might follow them through life.

About 10 that night Yip decided that his victim should be buried. He ordered the two men to carry out the body. Ah Wong demurred and fell to weeping on his bed, but Yip picked up the brush hook — a gesture that brought obedience. Chee-Chong and Ah Wong found a long pole and, lashing the dead man to it, carried him out. Main's dog was in a corner of the cabin where Yip killed it with the brush hook.

After Chee-Chong had dug the grave by lantern light, the dog's body was tossed in, but there was a problem with Main's body because Chee-Chong had merely dug a deep hole. Yip Luck hacked at the dead man's knees, doubled up his legs and dumped him in head first.

After more threats by Yip Luck, the three returned to the house. Yip Luck and Chee-Chong spent the rest of the night cleaning up the cabin, while Ah Wong lay on his bed trembling and occasionally weeping.

Toward morning, as the others slept, he slipped out of the cabin and hurried to Steveston. Here he told the whole ghastly story to his cousin who advised him to immediately leave. There was so much searching going on, however, that he didn't dare move.

Meanwhile, in his New Westminster cell Chung Chee-Chong had confirmed Wong's story. Shortly afterwards he died of tuberculosis. Ah Wong was charged with complicity in the murder of Alec Main. But to ensure his role as a Crown witness, no evidence was presented and a jury said "Not Guilty."

The next day saw the unusual courtroom spectacle of Yip Luck pleading guilty to murder — a man without counsel, whose plea was accepted. Judge Irving sentenced him to die on the gallows on November 16, 1900.

When November 16 arrived it was after many days of heavy rain which caused the trap door on the gallows to swell. When the executioner yanked the lever, nothing happened. He tried again and again. Then with a shrug, he looked at Sheriff Armstrong who stepped over and tentatively tried it. The trap crashed open and the startled Sheriff looked round to see only a taut and swaying rope where a second before the condemned man stood.

Yip Luck had unknowingly achieved two firsts: He was the first man in B.C. to plead guilty to murder, and the first to be accidentally hanged by a Sheriff instead of the official hangman.

Experienced policemen know that what seems logical on the surface can change dramatically during an investigation. Such was the result in

# The Case of the Kootenay Strangler

As the sun dipped behind the Monashee Mountains on the evening of June 4, 1902, it cast a shadow on a man called Henry Rose rowing a skiff toward the steamer landing at Nakusp on the west side of Upper Arrow Lake. With quick movements he tied up his boat and hurried away to find the local policeman.

Rose, a 64-year-old trapper and prospector, was a powerfully built man from his shoulders to the tips of his work-hardened fingers. In his 12 years in B.C. he had roamed all over the Kootenays in search of furs and gold. On this June evening, however, Rose wasn't concerned with mineral wealth. He was anxious to find the local Provincial Constable and unburden himself of a tale of horror and tragedy. It was a story that would be the topic of conversation in the Arrow Lakes region for months.

Constable for the district was 45-year-old Walter Scott. His detachment was one of a dozen that sprinkled the vast Kootenay country, supervised from Nelson by Chief Constable W. H. Bullock-Webster. In Nakusp's little frame police station at 8:30 that evening, Henry Rose told his story to the burly Constable Scott.

The community of Nakusp on Upper Arrow Lake, and the Leyland Hotel from where began the ill-fated trip down the lake.

Rose explained that just after midday, when he was having a drink in Nakusp's Leyland Hotel, he met two old prospecting buddies, Jack Cole and Nelson "Nels" Demar, one of the best liked prospectors in the Kootenays. Although Demar was small and approaching 80, he could still pack 50 pounds through the mountains with men 60 years younger. Like both Rose and Cole, he had a small holding a few miles down the lake from Nakusp.

Between drinks in the Leyland, Rose suggested that they go down to his place where he'd give them some seedling cabbages from his garden. Cole and Demar were not too keen, but a few more drinks changed their minds. Finally, they all headed for Rose's skiff. As the trio headed down the lake a stiff breeze sprang up and with it a nasty chop. In keeping with the unfriendly mood of the weather, Demar and Cole got into a heated argument. Finally Demar called Cole "the crookedest and meanest man on the lake."

To calm them down, Rose continued, he picked up a bottle of whisky and passed it around. They were about four miles south of Nakusp, still bucking wind and waves, when the bottle was passed again. After laboring at the oars for another 10 minutes, Cole remarked to Demar: "It's too far to row to Henry's place. Why don't we go ashore and make camp, and Harry can row down and bring the vegetables back."

They headed the skiff onto a sandy beach and all got out. While Demar made a fire, Cole walked along the foreshore. Rose, continuing with his story to Constable Scott, said that he pushed the boat out and started south again.

He was only a dozen yards from shore when his companions yelled

from the beach, "Aren't you going to leave us any whisky?" Rose said he replied: "Nothing doing. You've had enough."

Minutes later, however, he decided to improve relations by trying to catch a fish for the two men. As he rowed along he suddenly heard, borne on the wind, a cry for help. He paused and heard it again, and figured it must have come from his two friends.

Hastily pulling in his line, he turned and headed back, landing about 100 yards from where he had left them. He ran forward and saw Cole face down on the ground. When he turned him over, he was stunned to find that the man was dead. He had been struck by something, but what he couldn't say. Looking up, he noticed Demar about 20 yards away, swaying on his feet. He had both hands pressed to his face, blood trickling between his fingers.

Demar could only mutter something about two men coming out of the bush with clubs and attacking them. But, Rose continued to Constable Scott, he saw no signs of anyone nearby and suspected that his friends had got into a fight.

He wanted to bring Demar to Nakusp for treatment but the old prospector refused to go. "Just let me be." he said. "You go and get help."

Rose said that he made Demar as comfortable as possible near the fire. Then he replenished it with wood and rowed back to Nakusp. It was nearly 9 p.m. when Rose finished his story. Constable Scott immediately assembled three men to go with him and Rose to the bay. Two hours later they reached the scene of the killing.

In the light of a flickering stable lantern, Rose pointed out the body of Cole. Nearby lay Demar, semi-conscious and covered with blood. Constable Scott's quick examination showed that Cole lay on his back, a felt hat on his chest, protruding eyes staring skyward. Scott got the impression that he had been strangled. There was no time for further deliberation, however, for Demar needed immediate attention.

They roused him from his stupor, but all he muttered was a request that sounded like "leave me alone." It was apparent the old man didn't know where he was. Gently they lifted him down to the skiff, and by 2 a.m. he was being examined by a doctor. Demar's major injury was a blow over his right eye, so severe that he lost the sight. With Demar attended to, Scott returned to Cole's body with Rose and the coroner.

As Scott checked around he wondered, among other things, how the hat came to be on Cole's chest. Rose said he didn't put it there. It was now daybreak, enabling Scott to check for footprints. He saw none to bear out the story of men with clubs. There was only one club in evidence — a piece of edging about four feet long, probably washed up on the beach in a high wind. Maybe it had been used on Demar since one end was bloodstained. There were some handprints in blood along a log, showing where perhaps Demar had tried to crawl over it and failed. In the sand on the beach were two full bottles of whisky. It was strange, thought Scott, because Rose in his statement said that he had not given his friends any whisky when he left. The case was most mysterious.

Returning to Nakusp with Cole's body, Constable Scott quickly arranged for a medical examination and an inquest. From the doctor attending Demar he received grave news. "He's had a blow on the head in addition to his eye injury. At his age, I wouldn't hold out much hope for recovery. It'll be touch and go with him."

"Can he speak?" asked Scott. The doctor thought it might be all right to ask the old man a few questions.

By the old trapper's bedside, Constable Scott heard a story that contradicted Rose's account. They had rowed down the lake, said Demar in halting whispered sentences, and it was Cole and Rose who got into the argument. Finally Demar, thinking they might grapple and upset the boat, made the rising wind an excuse to turn in to shore.

"Had they been drinking in the boat?" asked Scott.

"Yes," said Demars. "They drank out of my bottle. I had the bartender pull the cork in the Leyland because we didn't have a corkscrew."

When they got to the beach, Demar continued, Rose in a rage took after Cole. Both hit the ground in a rough and tumble. Finally Rose got astride of Cole and began throttling him. Demar said that he circled the pair, then desperately tried to pull Rose from the motionless Cole.

"So you'd try to take his part!" yelled Rose, still in an uncontrollable temper. Struggling to his feet he rushed at Demar who tripped on a root and fell. Before he could rise, Rose had kicked him on his head. Half stunned, Demar got to his feet and, facing Rose, asked "What are you trying to do — kill me?"

Rose then clubbed him viciously over the right eye with the stick. Demar went down again, this time for good.

"Who lit the fire?" asked Scott.

"I lit it when we first landed," said Demar.

"Was the wind blowing up the lake all the time?"

"Yes, blew from the south all day long," said Demar.

There was a reason for the Constable's question. Rose had said the cry for help came downwind. The wind, in fact, was in the other direction.

Rose by now was a prime suspect insofar as the policeman was concerned. Then from the doctor he got the autopsy report on Cole. He had sustained a violent blow on the jaw from either a fist or a club, most likely a fist. Death, however, was really due to strangulation.

Scott pondered aloud the possibility of Demar strangling Cole, then tripping over something and injuring his eye on a piece of wood.

"He couldn't fall on top of his head," remarked the doctor, reminding Scott of the scalp wound in support of Demar's statement, "and he couldn't have strangled Cole after the eye injury. He would have been semi-conscious for quite a time."

Scott decided that Rose's story was fabrication and promptly arrested him for murder. It was weeks before Nels Demar was fit to give evidence. After a preliminary hearing, Rose was committed for trial.

On the scene by now was Chief Constable Bullock-Webster, along with Provincial Constable C. W. Young of Nelson and Constable Bob

Upper from Revelstoke. Their combined efforts produced, in conjunction with sketches, plans and photographs of the murder scene, an interesting case history of prisoner Rose.

Six years before the fight on the lakeside beach, the officers learned, Rose had got into a fight with his partner, James Ryan, on the Kootenay Lake steamer *Nelson.* Before the pair were separated, Rose had half strangled Ryan.

The next year with another partner, Charles Rose (no relation), Rose got into an argument in a Rossland bank about their share in a tie-cutting project. Henry Rose had pulled a knife. Charley got possession of the weapon, but only after a struggle. In August 1900, Rose had been fined $20 for choking a dance hall girl named May Cline. Again, in 1901, he had tried to strangle his friend Matt Whitlock.

At a reunion of old-timers, Walter Scott is identified by the arrow.

The sternwheeler *Nelson* where Rose tried to strangle his partner.

Later that year, the officers further learned, a trapper named C. H. Mann went with Demar and Rose to Demar's cabin. When Cole appeared, Rose picked a fight with him. When they were separated Rose muttered, "I'll fix you before the year's out."

There was, however, a lull in their enmity. In July that year, Demar took Rose along with Matt Whitlock and a man called Lawson to Cole's place on the lake shore. Soon another argument rose between Rose and Cole, and Rose left with Whitlock and Lawson.

Finally, in the fall of the same year, Customs Officer Leo Simmons pulled Rose off one Cecil West after a squabble in a barroom. "I had a tough time breaking his grip on West's throat," Simmons told the investigators. It seemed that whenever Rose had a few drinks he wanted to fight. With his big, powerful hands he always tried to choke his victims.

Early in October 1902, the Rose case came up in Nelson Assize Court before Chief Justice Gordon Hunter. Rose, seemingly unperturbed, still stuck to his original story. Despite a gruelling two-hour cross-examination, he didn't change it.

His counsel, while not emphasizing the possibility of the men with clubs coming out of the bush, laid down some strong hints that Demar could have strangled Cole, then fallen down and sustained the eye injury. Medical testimony of Doctors Cross and Carruthers of Revelstoke put this theory in doubt.

Chief Justice Hunter quietly played detective at one stage of Rose's cross-examination when he brought out a point that might have escaped attention. He asked the accused to identify something on Constable Young's sketch. When Rose put down the pencil, His Lordship remarked: "I see you're left-handed."

It was a point not lost on the jury. The injury to Demar's right eye was more than likely inflicted by a left-handed person.

During the gruelling two-day trial, the defence skirted the question of the prisoner's past character. This tactic effectively blocked the Crown from introducing some of the highlights of Rose's quarrelsome career. Only once did his past intrude. Crown Counsel W. A. Macdonald asked him how he knew that Cole was dead.

"I knew by looking at him," said Rose.

"But all men lying on the ground aren't dead," Macdonald pointed out. Then he added: "How did you know Matt Whitlock wasn't dead when you tried to strangle him in the Leyland Hotel?"

The jury deliberated just over four hours and their verdict was "guilty." Rose was sentenced to death.

At 8 o'clock on the bitterly cold morning of November 21, 1902, he walked firmly to the scaffold in the Nelson jail yard. There Henry Rose, who had choked life from one man and practiced on several more and a woman, felt a hangman's noose around his neck. It was far more unyielding than even his powerful fingers. As the crowd below momentarily lifted their hats, he plummeted downward.

# The Trapper's Return

**After the shooting he promised to return for the dusky Shuswap girl. He did — but not in the way she expected.**

In the late spring of 1909, a husky 20-year-old trapper named Ben Blakely decided to take a break from his Gun Creek trapline in the wild Bridge River Country and visit Lillooet. Ben, an American, found there were times when he had to break the isolated monotony of a trapper's life. True, there was one nearby social contact — the Thiverges on Gun Creek. Archie Thiverge, from Quebec, was a little, broken-down man in his mid-fifties addicted to home brew and bad language who packed to the mines. However, if Archie wasn't attractive, he had a common-law wife who was. She was a Shuswap Indian called Agnes.

Agnes led a lonely and austere life with Thiverge, and probably

The B.C. Provincial Police office in Fernie where Albert Hauser started the sequence that resulted in Ben Blakely standing trial in Clinton.

looked for consolation from the strapping young Blakely. Ben, it seems, was not averse to giving a little consolation, especially when Thiverge was absent with his pack train.

Of late, the Frenchman couldn't help noticing how Ben got preferential treatment with food. True, there was such a thing as backwoods hospitality, but this was different. Archie was suspicious, and beginning to feel that there was more to his wife's friendly welcome. A confrontation occurred one day in late May when Blakely stopped at the cabin on his way to Lillooet, a pack on his back, a rifle in his hand.

Whether or not it was because of Agnes, enmity between the two men had increased. Little things such as Archie blaming Ben for purposely forgetting his mail on a recent trip to Lillooet. Now, as Archie lolled in the doorway and viewed Blakely standing below the front steps, he commented negatively on Ben's ability as a trapper. Then he added a demand for $25 for horse hire.

"I never said I'd pay you $25," snorted Blakely.

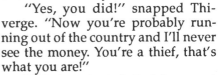

"Yes, you did!" snapped Thiverge. "Now you're probably running out of the country and I'll never see the money. You're a thief, that's what you are!"

Blakely retorted that he owed nothing. Finally, with one comment leading to another, Blakely told Thiverge what he thought of him, including his ill-treatment of Agnes.

At the mention of Agnes, Archie's eyes flickered with suspicious interest. Cursing, he turned, grabbed a Winchester leaning against the wall and pumped a shell into the breach. He faced Blakely whose own gun now covered the enraged Frenchman.

Agnes, sole witness to the scene, said later that Thiverge used his gun like a club. Rushing at Blakely he struck him a blow that knocked the young man sprawling. Before Archie could strike a second blow, Blakely rolled over on the ground and fired a shot that hit Thiverge in the chest. Thiverge sank to his knees, the gun falling from his grasp. Finally, he collapsed face down on the ground.

Shaken by this development, Agnes and Blakely then carried the

wounded man indoors and laid him on a bed. There wasn't much said, Agnes' Indian stoicism not lending itself to histrionics. "What'll you do now?" she asked quietly.

"I guess I'll have to get out of the country," was Blakely's reply. "But I'll send for you." He quickly embraced the girl and was gone.

Agnes then approached Thiverge and noticed he was still alive. She started down the trail to her brother's cabin half a mile away, but met an Indian who worked for a nearby placer miner. They hurried back to the cabin but Thiverge died a few minutes after they arrived.

In due course Lillooet coroner Caspar Phair held an inquest, and a warrant was issued for Ben Blakely. Provincial Constables Williams and Manson were already on his trail, after checking Blakely's cabin to make sure he hadn't returned. Then they tried another of his cabins seven miles away. There was evidence that it had been visited recently. The two Constables followed his tracks for 16 miles into the mountains practically to snow line. There the trail vanished.

Meanwhile, Chief Constable Joe Burr at Ashcroft with Constables Fitzgerald and Russell had also joined the search. In the days that followed, the police found a cabin broken into, with an axe, pair of moccasins and black mackinaw coat missing. Finally, after another week in the rugged Coast Mountains, the baffled searchers were sure of only one thing — Blakely was an expert bushman since no one else could have travelled so far in such short time.

Some idea of conditions encountered by the police is contained in the following extract from Burr's report to Victoria headquarters:

"...it's a terrible country to travel in after you leave the beaten trails, and owing to heavy storms previous to my going in, the fallen timber and underbrush were very thick, necessitating our cutting our way, for miles in places, to get through with saddle horses. We travelled in all about 180 miles on horseback...."

Finally, the search was called off. Burr came to the conclusion that Blakely had lashed logs together and crossed the river. After that he could skirt the mining camps above the south fork of Bridge River, then possibly go down Anderson and Harrison Lakes to the Harrison River. Here he could catch a CPR train to Vancouver. On this theory telegrams were sent to police posts and all border points. Despite the widespread alarm, nothing was heard of the fugitive. As the weeks merged into months the opinion was that Ben Blakely had perhaps met death in the mountains, a not unknown occurrence when even the most experienced men travelled alone.

The true story would have likely remained unknown had not a young miner named Albert C. Hauser become friends more than four years later with a fellow miner on Poor Man Creek in Montana. Albert Johnson, the man called himself, but later admitted to Hauser that his real name was Ben Blakely. Somewhere in the background, Blakely, it appeared, had a wife.

Whenever they exchanged confidences, however, Hauser noticed that he did most of the talking. Blakely was reticent about his past. In addition, Hauser noticed that whenever Canada was mentioned he changed the subject.

Finally, one night in the bunkhouse Blakely told Hauser about the shooting of Archie Thiverge and the desperate flight from justice through the formidable Lillooet Mountains. Afterwards, Hauser suggested Blakely cross the border and give himself up. Ben, however, was sure the Canadian courts would not view his story with any credence.

"You don't know that country," he told Hauser. "Up there they'll hang you as soon as look at you."

"But there's that Indian girl," said Hauser. "If she saw it all, she'd be a good witness for you."

Blakely shook his head. What was past was past, and he wasn't resuscitating it.

Hauser was not only a friend, however, but a persistent one. That fall when he happened to be in Fernie, B.C., he visited A. C. Minty, District Head of the B.C. Police. By coincidence, Minty had been stationed at Ashcroft at the time of the Blakely search. He took a description of Hauser's Montana friend, then rummaged through the back circulars until he found Ben Blakely's wanted poster.

Hauser swore to his statement, and U.S. Marshal McKay of Butte, Montana, arrested Blakely. Eventually, Blakely was extradited to Canada and in the spring of 1914 appeared before Mr. Justice Denis Murphy at the Clinton Assize.

The case was weak, the evidence of the sole witness, Agnes, strongly in favor of Blakely. Finally, His Lordship said to Moore, the Crown counsel: "Do you think, Mr. Moore, it's worth while going to the jury on this evidence?"

"It certainly looks as if I couldn't ask for a verdict of murder," replied Moore.

"I think on the woman's evidence it is a clear case of self defence," Justice Murphy summarized.

"Well, speaking as a man of the West," said Moore, "I can hardly blame the accused for having shot after what happened."

"Seems to me," said the Cariboo-born Judge, "that if the accused had not shot he would have been a dead man."

"I'm willing to concede a dismissal of the prosecution," Moore answered.

"You are discharged," said Judge Murphy to Blakely.

The best pleased person in the courtroom seemed to be the dusky Agnes, whose evidence had swung the scales of justice in favor of her friend, Ben. Although he hadn't sent for her as promised, he was here now.

She went over and impulsively took his hand. "I'm glad you're back, Ben," she said with a smile. "You said you would return."

If there was anything more to add to this happy occasion she waited for Ben to say it.

Ben did. He led her gently to the back of the courtroom where a young woman sat with a baby. As she stood, Ben turned to Agnes and said: "I would like you to meet my wife."

# The Parking Ticket
# that Killed Three People

Prince Rupert — what a dull place to spend their "Glorious Fourth of July" thought the U.S. sailors. No fireworks. No excitement. A taxi driver tragically provided both.

In the 1930s British Columbia's port of Prince Rupert was not only the western terminus for fishing fleets and the Canadian National Railway, but also headquarters for policing a vast wilderness empire roughly described as northwestern B.C. In the Provincial Courthouse 45-year-old Division Inspector William "Big Bill" Service, veteran of 25 years in the B.C. Police, supervised the biggest police division in Western Canada. It was giant "D" Division that extended from Rivers Inlet north to the Yukon, and inland over 150 miles to Hazelton. Or-

Top Left: William "Big Bill" Service, seated, when he was a Sergeant and, at his left shoulder, Constable George H. Clark who would one day shoot his murderer.

Opposite: Prince Rupert, showing the dock area where Gurvich was given a parking ticket and the courthouse — in the horseshoe crescent — where he murdered two policemen.

Below: The Royal Hotel, scene of the Wild West shoot-out.

derly room Sergeant in the Division Office was another police old-timer, 50-year-old Bob Gibson.

Here and there were dotted police detachments, and along the coast patrol boats that did police and coastguard service. One such boat operated out of Prince Rupert, a 75-foot diesel craft skippered by Corporal Harold Raybone. On this July 4, 1939, morning he was just in from a patrol.

As the Corporal piloted the diesel cruiser into Prince Rupert harbor, he noticed a U.S. destroyer, the *Hopkins,* had tied up during his absence. Thus the American Fourth of July holiday found U.S. sailors crowding Prince Rupert sidewalks, occasionally remarking that it didn't seem at all like the Glorious Fourth. They missed the bands, the parades, and especially the fireworks. Around two that afternoon the Royal Hotel beer parlor was packed by the U.S. sailors, including those who lamented the lack of fireworks. They were soon to experience a display that none ever forgot.

It started a few blocks down the street when taxi driver Mike Gurvich drove up to Jack McNulty's Hardware Store. He showed McNulty a .38 revolver bullet. "Got any like this?"

"A .38 Special," mused McNulty. "Sure we've got them."

"Gimme a box."

McNulty passed over the shells and Mike Gurvich drove off. He and his two older brothers ran a taxi stand and bowling alley. On this July morning when Mike had got to work a police summons awaited him, left by Corporal George H. Clark. The summons related to improper parking at the Canadian National dock. Though there was a place on the dock for taxis, Mike, in spite of police warnings, had persisted in parking illegally.

Maybe defying the police order made him feel important. Or maybe he felt he was being persecuted. Five years before he'd been a patient in a mental hospital. Whatever the case, the summons made him very angry. He phoned his lawyer.

"They left this when I was out," he argued, "that ain't no legal service, is it?"

"Might as well take it, Mike," counselled his lawyer. "They can always come round with another … and find you in."

The answer didn't satisfy Gurvich. The more he thought about it, the more hostile he became. He was fed up with cops, fed up with being told where to park his taxi. Later that morning he confronted Corporal Clark.

"You didn't serve that summons properly," he argued, "and you ain't going to see me in no court!"

"You got the summons in your pocket now?" asked Clark mildly, well aware of Gurvich's attitude to law enforcement.

"Sure I have."

"Well, you just keep note of the date. I'll see you in court."

Gurvich shot him a look of distaste. Then, convinced that he was the victim of arbitrary police power, he jumped in his car and drove away. His first stop was McNulty's Hardware Store where he bought the .38 revolver ammunition.

About this time Corporal Raybone was on his way to the courthouse. He was only 200 yards away when he met logger Harvey Dumas. As they chatted on the street corner, Raybone noticed Mike Gurvich in his taxi heading toward the courthouse. In a minute or two, while he still talked, he noticed Gurvich again, heading back to town at a fair speed.

While the two talked, inside the courthouse Corporal D. W. Taylor thought he heard a series of muffled explosions somewhere along the basement corridor. He got up from his typewriter and looked up and down the passage, glimpsing a man disappearing up the stairs at the end of the hall. There was an eerie silence in the building. Taylor, still puzzled by the noises he had heard, walked past the open door of the Division Office. Just when he concluded that the reports had come from the street, he heard a low sound, like a groan, coming from the Division Office.

He walked over to the counter. Behind it was an unbelievable sight. Sergeant Gibson lay on the floor in a pool of blood, a bullet hole in the back of his head. Then Taylor saw a pair of feet sticking out from behind a desk. It was Inspector Service. He also had been shot in the head.

Taylor hastily looked around. Two chairs were overturned. From the position of one of them he figured Gibson had been sitting at his typewriter when an assailant cut him down with a single shot. But was it a single shot? Taylor had heard four explosions, in pairs. Looking round he saw a bullet hole in the floor, another in the wall.

Then unable to see a phone he dashed to his own office. On the way the thought struck him that the man he'd seen ducking around the corner must have fired the shots. But why? After phoning for help he ran into the hall where he met Corporal Raybone. Both men ran to the Division Office. Raybone knelt by the prone men. Suddenly he said: "Gibson's alive."

Just then from upstairs appeared two civil servants. They had heard shots. They were both sure the only person they had seen leaving the courthouse afterwards was Mike Gurvich. Then Raybone remembered he'd also seen Gurvich going to and from the courthouse in his car. At the most, his stay could only have been a minute or two.

At that moment Corporal Clark and Constable Terry Stewart arrived. There was a hurried consultation, broken off when Raybone remarked: "If it was Gurvich ... we'd better find him ... and quick!"

There was a note of harsh finality in the sea-going policeman's voice.

While Taylor stood waiting for the doctor and ambulance, Clark, Raybone and Stewart leaped into a police car and headed for Gurvich's taxi stand near the Royal Hotel. He might be there, or in the living quarters at the back.

Gurvich, in the meantime, had pulled up opposite the Royal where fellow taxi driver Rosario Mazzei saw him get out of his car, gun in hand.

"I got 'em!" was Gurvich's triumphant shout.

"Got who?"

"I got Service and Gibson ... got 'em both!" shouted Gurvich as he disappeared, gun in hand, into the beer parlor crowded with U.S. sailors.

"Gimme a beer," he snapped at a waiter.

The waiter, eyeing the gun, hastily complied. Gurvich gulped the beer, pausing only to stand on tiptoe to look over the curtains onto the street. Muttering incoherent threats, he yelled again, "Gimme another beer."

By now nearby sailors were taking an interest in the excited customer who stood gulping beer, gun in hand.

Gurvich suddenly slammed down his half-empty glass and headed for the side door. As he crossed the street, a police car swung round the corner and pulled to a tire-screeching halt. The three officers leaped from the car. Gurvich eyed them, gun in hand.

Terry Stewart, in plainclothes and unarmed since it was his day off, did the logical thing. He used the car as a screen. Raybone and Clark, guns drawn, advanced on the killer. As Gurvich backed toward the Royal Hotel, Clark shouted at him to drop his gun. The answer was a shot.

Both Raybone and Clark fired, and so did Gurvich again.

Clark said later he thought that if Gurvich fired four shots in the courthouse, and two on the street, his gun might be empty. It was a vain hope. Gurvich had reloaded.

Gurvich backed from the advancing police through the beer parlor door.

Raybone quickly said to Clark: "Keep him busy here and I'll slip round to the other door and block him."

Before he could move, however, both officers saw Gurvich watching them from inside. Both fired simultaneously. Gurvich's head snapped back — a bullet between his eyes. His body crumpled among the patrons already on the floor — sailors from the U.S.S. *Hopkins* who had mourned that Prince Rupert had no fireworks on the Fourth of July!

Sergeant Gibson, meanwhile, had been moved to the hospital. He never regained consciousness. Inspector Service had died instantly. He left a wife and five young daughters.

At a coroner's inquest a few days later ballistic evidence linked Gurvich's gun with the double killing, and the jury praised the swift and courageous action of the police trio who had caught the killer. From Victoria Headquarters a month later came promotions for Clark, Raybone and Stewart.

The question has often been asked: Why did Gurvich murder Service and Gibson? No one knows.

# The Sharpshooter's Grudge

**In the wilderness of the Coast Mountains the
Indian war hero's reaction to the new provincial game
regulations resulted in murder.**

Professional big-game guides are usually a rugged breed and Frank
Gott followed the pattern. In fact he was one of the ruggedest. A full-
blooded Lillooet Indian, he got his unusual surname from his stern,
German-born stepfather, but his quick eye and vast knowledge of
game life was a direct legacy from his Indian father.

Without an ounce of surplus flesh, Frank was something akin to
an eagle — at his best in the mountains under a wide, blue sky. No one
ever had a clue to his age, for like most Indians reaching a certain stage
of life he seemed ageless. Of his prowess in
the bush there were stories aplenty. He
could make 40 miles a day and often
packed 135 pounds. But then he was
young, now he wasn't.

One late afternoon in early October
1932, as the sun dipped behind the
9,000-foot mountain ramparts west of
Bridge River, Frank Gott was trudging
along a trail high above a valley that lay
wrapped in the first crisp chill of
fall. There was another chill in
the air that only Frank felt, and it
held a deeper meaning. It was
the chill of death — his death.
He was in the last stages of
tuberculosis. With tired and
stumbling steps, he finally
reached a fallen log and rested,
wracked by occasional spasms of
coughing. Fumbling in his
pocket, he found a dirty piece
of paper and with the stub
of a pencil wrote:

"Still alive but my
time will soon come ...
old enough ... take good

Frank Gott who served as a
sniper in France during World
War One until authorities
learned that he was over 60,
not the 47 he claimed to be.

care of Jim, Blackie and the Big Kid, Tommy Horse. Come pretty close before ... done ... deed him."

Then came another attack of coughing. Stuffing the scrap of paper in his pocket, with an effort he got to his feet and struggled on. Most of what he had written is difficult to interpret, but his past career gives a clue to one phrase: "Come pretty near before." Maybe he was thinking of a trip to Tete Jaune Cache in 1894 when he had almost starved to death; or maybe his thoughts took him back to Flanders and the mud, fear and fury of World War One.

It was in the spring of 1916 that Frank Gott dyed his whitening hair and donned a khaki uniform to train with No. 3 Company of the 102nd Battalion, Canadian Expeditionary Force. His Company Commander was Captain A. J. Matthews who would become Vancouver's crusty City Archivist. It was Captain Matthews who originated their ultimate name "North British Columbians," and Colonel Warden who designed their cap badge. It featured the profile of an Indian in feathered headdress. Frank Gott was the model.

He was an outstanding soldier, this aging Indian, according to those who served with him. Once, in training camp in England, an officer was overhead to remark: "Where did we pick up that old fellow?"

Gott answered the cutting remark with a unique challenge — a 10-mile run against anyone in the battalion. There were no takers.

Later, at the front, in a hellfire corner aptly dubbed Shelly Lane, No. 3 Company was clinging to bare existence under the deadly concussion of German shells. A young officer, scrambling cautiously from one bomb bay to another to see how the troops were surviving, came upon the swarthy-featured man from Lillooet.

"Scared?" yelled the officer, with an attempt at a grin.

"Not me!" yelled back the unshaken Gott, adding the quip, "I wouldn't have missed it for anything!"

After that, they made Gott a sniper. Tirelessly, he would lie in the debris of French farmhouses waiting for a glimpse, through his telescopic sight, of any stray Germans. It was nothing new to Frank. In the mountains around Lillooet he had often waited with the same skill and patience for mountain sheep or goat. Allied to his marksmanship was always the patience of his Indian forebears.

Then the army all but broke his heart. He was told he was too old, and was being sent home. He pleaded to stay with the battalion. Clutching the hand of Matthews — a major by now — in his traditional Indian two-handed grip, he vowed he was still as good as any man. But the ruling stuck. Gott was sent home. Matthews later said that Gott was 62, undoubtedly the oldest Allied soldier on active service.

He returned to Lillooet, supremely proud of his adventures in France, prouder still of his khaki uniform and his cap with the Indian-face badge. For years after his discharge, while he acted as a big-game guide trailing his trio of packhorses out of Lillooet, he continued to wear his army cap.

Tragically, in 1930 he shot a bear out of season and Game Warden

Albert Farey unexpectedly rode into Gott's camp. Farey in his career had been a game guide and served 12 years in the B.C. Provincial Police before transferring to the Game Department. In addition, like Gott, he was a World War One veteran.

Frank Gott was fined for his breach of the law and bore Farey an undying grudge.

Two years later the tragedy was compounded. In early October Gott was hunting with Jimmy Dalton and 14-year-old Raymond Miller, both of Lillooet. Late in the afternoon they started making camp above Bridge River, about 26 miles from Lillooet. Just as Dalton got the fire going, Farey rode into their midst.

Spotting a fresh deerskin beside the tent, Farey dismounted and walked over to it. This was the first year that deer tags were used in B.C., an innovation that some old-timers considered a little cramping.

"Where's the tag?" Farey asked Gott as he fingered the hide.

The answer came not from Gott, but from Gott's rifle. The Game Warden's back was the target, and that's where two bullets caught him.

As Farey slumped to the ground, Dalton and Miller sprang to their feet, shocked at the cold-blooded killing. Unmoved, Gott handed his gun to Dalton, then said to Miller: "You can have my horse, I'm done for."

He turned and walked toward a grove of pine and disappeared.

Miller and Dalton examined the Game Warden. He was dead. Then one of them hurried to the nearest settlement, Moha, to alert the police.

**Frank Gott was the model for the Indian profile
on the cap badge of the North British Columbians.**

District Sergeant Henry Wood quickly mobilized a squad of police and game wardens to track down the killer. One thing the police well realized — Gott would be a difficult man to find with his wide knowledge of the Lillooet country. If he had a gun they would be up against a dead shot who had already murdered a man when his back was turned. What the police did not know was Gott's tuberculosis. In addition, he was still suffering the effects of a narrow escape from death two months before when a PGE train had trapped him on his horse in a narrow rock cut at Seton Lake. Although Gott suffered only cuts and bruises, his horse was killed.

Planning their pursuit, the police and Game Wardens fanned out on Gott's possible trail. Game Department Sergeant Robert Robertson and Game Warden Joseph Quesnel were detailed to watch the Bridge River. At dusk three days later, they saw their man.

On a high bank of bare, sandy hillside above the river the two walked to halt the fugitive. As they approached, they glimpsed something in his hand. At 90 feet in the evening light it was hard to say what it was: perhaps a revolver, maybe a knife.

Robertson, rifle in hand, called on Gott to surrender. The answer was linked with Gott's proud army days. "I'm a soldier, and I never surrender."

"I'm a soldier, too," said Robertson calmly. "The best thing you can do is to throw that thing away and give yourself up. If you don't, I'm liable to shoot."

"If you shoot, I'll shoot too!" said Gott. As he spoke he advanced on Quesnel, brandishing what they now saw was a hunting knife. Robertson fired a warning shot into the ground. Startled, Gott whirled and disappeared over the high bank. The Game Warden ran to the edge to see their man bounding downhill in a trail of dust.

He was heading for a rock cut. Robertson and Quesnel fired two more warning shots in the air. They didn't stay his flight. As Gott reached the rock, Robertson fired again. Gott fell. The two wardens rushed downhill and as they reached Gott's side, saw that he was intent on suicide. He had the hunting knife at his throat. Quesnel rushed up and grabbed it.

The shots summoned other members of the posse who quickly took Gott to Lillooet. From there he was taken to the hospital at Lytton, where he died that evening. He had a superficial leg wound which Dr. Ployart said had no direct bearing on his death. Tuberculosis was the real killer.

When word of Frank Gott's death spread, it aroused feelings of resentment. The police had hunted Frank Gott down and killed him — that was the theme. Only secondary, it seemed, was sympathy for Ed Farey or his widow. What wasn't generally known was that Bob Robertson — a sniper with the 28th Battalion where he served from October 1914 to March 1918 — was one of the best rifle shots in B.C. He could kill, disable or miss a fleeing man at will. He had deliberately missed Gott, the fragment of bullet taken from his leg had ricocheted off the rock wall.

In the dead man's pocket was found his final message — or rather, messages: One read:

"He has been watching me once too often. I am going to expire myself. It's all off with me anyway. Goodbye to all my friends. I am sorry but I done it. Fixed the game warden. He had no business to bother me like that. So long boys."

The other was a more cryptic missive:

"Artie, you were a friend once, but not now. You were the fault when the dead man arrested me three years ago, not getting my firearms, prospector, and etc. So long, we might meet but it's doubtful.

Joe Quesnel related later that when he was helping to pack Gott out of the hills there was a moment at a rest point when Gott looked at him steadily and remarked:

"If I could have got across the river to some Indian friends, I could have got a gun and some ammunition and shot as many policemen as I could."

"And then what?" asked Quesnel.

"Then," said the white-haired Gott, "I'd get to a graveyard where some of my people are buried, and there I would shoot myself."

A day or so later, a jury of Lillooet townsmen reached this verdict about the death of Frank Gott:

"We find that Frank Gott came to his death at Lytton on October 5, 1932, as a result of shock following a gunshot wound from a ricochet bullet, the wound itself not being sufficient to cause death, inflicted by game wardens, while the deceased was attempting to escape as a fugitive from justice. We exonerate the game wardens from any blame in the matter and find the Provincial Police rendered every assistance to the deceased after the injury was received by him."

Despite the evidence, the controversy continued. Gott's old army comrades voiced opinions, while editorials in Coast papers loudly charged that his death had been unnecessary. In Lillooet there was a mass meeting one night, resulting in a petition to Attorney-General Harry Pooley to re-open the enquiry.

Replied Pooley, in effect: "It is open to anyone to lay a charge of manslaughter against the game wardens. But after reading the inquest depositions I'm certain that, from a legal point of view, there would be no chance of conviction."

Finally the controversy waned. During the furor, however, few glances were directed at Ed Farey's grave — or sympathy offered his sorrowing wife.

# Nobody Wanted
# to Hang the Little Sailor

**In 1872 ex-sailor George Bell was the first white man to
be hanged on Vancouver Island. But the question remains —
Did justice prevail?**

Departure Bay at Nanaimo is familiar to tens of thousands of B.C. residents and visitors who travel to Vancouver Island aboard B.C. Ferries. It is a busy place, the huge vessels arriving and leaving with clockwork precision, seaplanes skimming to a landing, and thousands of pleasure boats shuttling from Nanaimo's harbor to the nearby productive sportfishing waters. Departure Bay, in fact, has been a popular waterway for centuries.

First came the Indians, including the war-like Haida who paddled massive cedar canoes southward from their Queen Charlotte Islands homeland, murdering and pillaging their way southward to what is today Washington. The wild Euclataws from Desolation Sound camped here, noses and lips pierced by bone ornaments, some addicted to cannibalism. They — and other Indian tribes — owned slaves who were killed at their master's whim, with special clubs to do it. But not only Indians have died here.

When the white men started mining local coal over a century ago, the Bay was a haven for sailing ships waiting to load from Dunsmuir's

wharf. Here, hauled by the first locomotives west of the Great Lakes, freight cars daily brought 20,000 tons of coal. Here, too, in 1872 two men fought a death duel of incredible savagery.

One of them was George Bell, a sailor on HMS *Satellite* when she dropped anchor in Esquimalt in 1857. The next summer, when some 50,000 men stampeded to the Fraser River where gold had been discovered, he deserted. He was one of many sailors who rebelled at the brutal whippings and slave-like conditions common to British warships. He crossed into Washington, but four years later returned to become a miner in Nanaimo's Douglas pit.

A quiet-spoken man with grey-blue eyes and fair hair, Bell was of slight build, although navy life had tightened his muscles. He was a hard worker and lived alone in a cabin near the mine. He hadn't given much thought to women until the spring of 1869 when he met Annie Iwhat, a pretty 16-year-old Indian girl. In those days it wasn't unusual for a white man to have an Indian wife, although frequently it was a "blanket marriage" rather than a legal one. But to George Bell, a staunch Wesleyan, there was no question about simply living together and they were legally married.

For the next few years, the cabin in the clearing near the Douglas pit was a bright and sunny place for George Bell, sunnier still after two baby girls appeared. Three happy years passed quickly. Then, on June 21, 1872, came disaster.

At the pithead that morning George discovered he had left his coffee can at home. He returned for it, but found the children alone. Thinking Annie had gone to feed the chickens, he wandered down the

Nanaimo in the 1870s as George Bell knew it, and Dunsmuir Wharf where he killed the man who had seduced his wife.

fence line. There he saw something that made his eyes harden. From the nearby cabin of bachelor miner Tom Datson, Annie appeared. As she approached, George could see by her glazed look and stumbling step that she had been drinking.

Hot and angry words were exchanged. From Annie's morose admissions George got the full impact of the ugly truth. Annie, it seems, had on more than one occasion succumbed to Datson. In his thirties, he was a big, raw-boned man with quite a reputation among the local women. Bell, rage in his heart, strode to his cabin.

"Get out of this neighborhood in 24 hours or I'll kill you!" was his brief but deadly threat.

Datson didn't argue. Something in the small man's eye, some glint of purposeful moral strength, made him wary. That afternoon Datson drew his pay at the mine, locked his cabin and headed for Nanaimo. He made the rounds of a few pubs and as he drank boasted of his exploits with Annie Bell. A day or two later he left for Departure Bay to see his cousin who got him a job at the coal wharf.

It wasn't long before word of Datson's bar-room bragging reached the Douglas pit and George Bell. Next day he remarked to a fellow miner: "I'm going to kill that Datson." Tragically, he soon demonstrated that he meant exactly what he said.

On June 25, four days after his ultimatum to Datson, Bell did not report for work. Immediately two of his friends, Charlie Alport and Jimmy Beck, hastened to find him. By now Bell had traced Datsun to the Departure Bay coal wharf. The ex-sailor was armed with a double-barreled shotgun, a hunting knife and a Colt revolver.

Enquiring for Datson, he was told that he was probably up at the Hughes house. There Bell headed, shotgun in hand, gun and knife in his belt. At the Hughes house he kicked open the door. Covering the wide-eyed Joe Hughes with the shotgun, he snapped: "Where's Datson?"

Hughes daughter, Mary, equally astonished, falteringly enquired: "What do you want him for?"

"I'm going to kill him," was his quiet reply.

At that moment Bell spotted Datson coming up the trail. With a warning look at Hughes, he put his finger to his lips. Suddenly, as the shotgun momentarily wavered, Hughes yelled, "Look out, Tommy!"

Bell charged through the door. He blasted both barrels at Datson who ducked in time to escape injury. Tossing the gun aside, Bell drew his revolver. As Datson dodged from tree to tree, Bell advanced, firing until his gun was empty. With the sound of the clicking of the empty weapon, Datson showed himself. Bell quickly shoved the gun in his belt and withdrew the razor-sharp hunting knife. He charged Datson.

Datson tried to throw Bell over his shoulder, but in mid-air Bell slashed the knife across Datson's back. With a grunt Datson pitched forward, still full of fight. In the seconds that followed, the pair were locked in a desperate, clawing encounter on the ground, Datson striving to hold off Bell's hand and the fearsome seven-inch blade. For minutes it seemed that Datson's size was of no avail against Bell's savage rage. Finally he managed to gain possession of the knife and with a heave was on top of Bell. Gasping for breath, half fainting from the loss of blood, Datson taunted: "You came to kill me, George, but now I'm going to kill you."

The words spurred Bell. He grabbed the knife with his bare hand and with a bone-cracking wrench flipped Datson. The knife flew from their grip. Bell grabbed the revolver from his belt. While it was useless as a firearm, it was still useful as a club. With terrible ferocity, he began to club Datson's face.

He stopped only when the revolver fell apart. Datson, with jaws broken, was now whimpering for mercy through toothless, bleeding gums. But there was no mercy in George Bell that afternoon. Snatching up the abandoned knife he slashed and stabbed.

Finally, his anger spent, he left his victim in a welter of blood and staggered toward the beach. He almost fell into the arms of Alport and Beck who had arrived by canoe, too late to head off the confrontation. Between Bell's sobs they heard his story, then went up the trail to pick up Datson and carry him to a canoe. The party headed for Nanaimo. On the way, Datson, in a delirious moment, imagined Bell was still after him and tried to scramble out of the canoe. Fearful of it upsetting, Alport and Beck held him down. Soon after, Datson died.

At Nanaimo there was an inquest and Bell was arrested for murder. Less than a month later, in July 1872, the little ex-sailor faced Chief Justice Matthew Baillie Begbie and a Nanaimo jury.

During the trial a succession of witnesses told of hearing Bell's threats or of seeing him at Departure Bay. All confirmed, however, that he was a man of previously good character. William Hunter testified to seeing Bell excited and crying, saying he would kill Datson. "But Bell was a good, peaceable man," he added. "I worked with him."

Even Joe Hughes who had faced Bell's shotgun gave testimony to the killer's good nature. Dr. Jones described Datson's injuries, and added that he had attended the birth of Bell's children and was struck with "how attentive and kind Bell was to his wife."

Jimmy Beck, who had known Bell for eight years, said that the day before the murder, when he met Bell, the latter had been weeping. He heard him say in a low tone: "My heart is broken ... keep away from me ... I think I'm going mad."

John Bryden said that when he was talking to Bell, the ex-sailor suddenly clenched his fist. Looking to the sky, he said: "There's a something ... something, urging me to kill that man!"

Bell's lawyer, George Bishop, put up a spirited defence for his client, even though he had been given inadequate time to prepare a defence. He had requested an adjournment to the Fall Assize, but Judge Begbie refused. Finally, after much argument he was given one extra day, but the Chief Justice remarked: "All the statements you want to study could be analyzed in an hour!"

In his defence presentation to the court, Bishop contrasted Bell's happy married life with Datson's infamous behaviour. When he told the court of Datson's boasting about seducing Annie, Bell sobbed.

Until 1902 hangings in Canada were
public, typified by the one above in
Eastern Canada in the late 1890s.
When Bell was hanged at Victoria's
Bastion Square Jail, 150 people were
invited into the courtyard to watch.

Finally, when John Schofield took the stand, Bishop brought out evidence that Schofield had seen Datson and Annie coming out of a patch of brush together. Here Chief Justice Begbie broke in on the examination with a sharp reminder: "This is useless, Mr. Bishop! I shall tell the jury that the evidence you are producing is immaterial!"

"I had hoped it would be in the way of palliation, My Lord," was Bishop's quiet explanation.

"It might be in New York!" snapped Begbie.

In his summing up, however, the Chief Justice had in mind the question of compassion for the prisoner. He said: "Wounded feelings are not an excuse for wilful murder. If you believe that he was sane enough to know that he was in violation of the law, you must convict him. On the other hand, if you believe that he was insane at the time, you must acquit him."

He concluded by complimenting Bishop for his handling of a difficult defence. After an hour's deliberation, the jury found Bell guilty.

Red-eyed and trembling, Bell had nothing to say as he stood to hear Begbie intone the death sentence in all its awesome finality: "...hanged by the neck until you are dead and may God have mercy on your soul."

Bell, stepping from the prisoner's box, seemed to hear that phrase ringing in his head. In a low, anguished outburst he echoed "...and may God have mercy on my soul."

Bell was scheduled to hang on November 5 in the stockaded prison yard at Victoria's Bastion Square Jail. While he waited out his four-month ordeal, controversy stirred the citizens of Victoria and Nanaimo. The issue was the matter of clemency or death for Bell, the press and the public with different opinions.

It was the Victorian era with its attitudes and platitudes; the era of "the rich man in his castle, the poor man at his gate." To many there was no acceptable excuse for human frailty — at least outside the gate! Nevertheless, some of the citizens "outside of the gate" started a petition urging a commutation of sentence.

Said a letter signed Justice in the *Colonist* newspaper at Victoria: "Datson was bad, granted. Bell orders him to leave and he obeys. Then, long after the murderer's blood has time to cool ... he follows him! Look at the mutilation of the body! Why, the murderer revelled in blood and cut, gashed, hacked and pounded the insensate form of his wretched victim until it bore little semblance to a human being! This is the man for whom mercy is asked! This is the man in whose behalf our citizens are asked to sign a petition for executive clemency! Were Bell's neck to escape the rope, capital punishment should be abolished in the Dominion!"

In answer came Mercy's letter in the *Victoria Standard*: "This letter must have been written by the hangman."

Another reader, signed Justice for All, noted: "If Datson hadn't crowed over the dishonor he'd done, Bell wouldn't have been a murderer."

Cornishman said it was "an unjust conviction, and Bell should have been allowed more time to prepare his defence."

In the meantime, George Bell sat in his Bastion Square cell, reading, talking to an occasional Nanaimo visitor and gaining comfort from the visits of Reverend William Pollard. As the day of execution approached the Jail Warden began looking for a hangman. His search presented an unexpected problem.

The reason was that although B.C. had been part of Confederation for some 18 months, there was no direct route to Eastern Canada and the official hangman. As a consequence, the Warden followed the past custom of going down the cell block in Bastion Square prison asking each prisoner if he wanted the job. Anyone who volunteered had his sentence automatically cancelled.

No prisoner volunteered, even to escape harsh jail conditions which included breaking rock all day while wearing 14-pound leg irons which were rivetted on when the prisoner entered jail and not removed until his release. For variation he could be chained to other convicts and, still wearing the leg irons, repair streets for up to 12 hours a day. The other 12 hours he spent in his cell, not much bigger than a cupboard, without light or plumbing. The food matched the rest of the harsh treatment, a pint of cornmeal gruel and eight ounces of bread morning and evening, with dinner the same except for a small ration of meat.

All an inmate had to do to gain freedom was pull a lever, knowing full well that even if he refused, the sailor would still hang. Nobody volunteered. Bell's fellow prisoners obviously felt that the hanging was an injustice. The Warden had to go outside the prison for his hangman.

Finally, came 6:30 on the morning of November 5. Bell, who had slept fitfully, arose to wash and dress. He was quite calm, and wanted only a cup of tea for breakfast. Then the prison blacksmith came to knock off his leg-irons with hammer and chisel, and minutes later the hangman entered to tie his hands behind his back. Bell, noticing how he fumbled, remarked with a smile, "Nervous?"

The hangman nodded.

At 8 a.m., as was the custom, a guard opened the stockade gate and invited the public in. About 150 people entered to watch the hanging. Then Bell walked firmly to the scaffold.

With no sign of nervousness he climbed the steps. As he stood on the platform a black hood was placed over his head and a hangman's noose around his neck. Then the hangman, also wearing a black hood, pulled the lever. George Bell died.

As a brisk and chilly wind whipped in from the harbor, the crowd slowly dispersed. Finally, only lawyer George Bishop remained. He waited the required hour before Bell could be cut down. Then he claimed the body and buried the little sailor at his own expense.

With three bullets in his head the man had
obviously been murdered. Persistent police work,
however, uncovered the improbable truth about

# The Man Who Couldn't Die

The strange sequence of events began on April 22, 1898. At the time
Vancouver was a sprawling scene of framed dwellings, horse-drawn
traffic churning muddy roads and, around the shore of False Creek,
acres of stumps. But times were good and near the waterfront three-
and four-story buildings made the beginnings of a Vancouver skyline.
The Yukon gold rush had spurred demands for supplies, and along
the docks was a forest of masts as windjammers from around the world
waited their turn to load at Hastings Mill.

South of the townsite was farmland, and across the wooden bridge
which spanned False Creek a wagon road cut through the bush and
over the height of land to the Fraser River. On this particular Friday
afternoon, four miles south of Vancouver, one man was completely un-
concerned about Vancouver's present, its future or, for that matter, its
past.

He lay face down in an abandoned chicken house on the old Mc-
Rorie Ranch. He was dead — and he was to present the B.C. Provincial Police with one of the weirdest cases it ever investigated.

The McRorie place was on River Road. The original owner had

Vancouver in the early 1890s. At the bottom right corner is the
intersection of Georgia and Granville Streets.

been killed by an Indian two years before and Henry Mole had taken over. On this particular afternoon he was looking for a pitchfork. He tried the door of the windowless chicken house, noticing that the outside staple that usually fastened the door had been withdrawn. When he pushed against the door he felt an obstruction. Pushing harder, he dislodged a stick that had been propped against the door on the inside. As his sight adjusted to the gloomy interior, he could see something lying on the floor.

By the light of matches, Mole made out that it was a man — and that he was dead. A pile of straw covered with grain sacks in one corner had evidently been used as a bed. Touching nothing, Mole left quickly, fastening the door with a staple. He saddled a horse and rode into New Westminster to inform the Provincial Police.

A few hours later Chief Constable R. B. Lister and Coroner Dr. Alfred Poole arrived. They examined the scene carefully. Dr. Poole estimated that the dead man was in his early forties. He was about 5' 9", had a short black beard and dark hair slightly greying at the sides.

He was fairly well dressed in a blue serge suit, black cotton shirt, and elastic-sided Congress shoes. One arm was folded beneath him, the other spread out. A cloth cap was on the back of his head, while his face rested against a small stump protruding through the earth floor.

There was no weapon in sight, no bloodstains. Lying on the floor was one ominous clue to the stranger's death — a little cardboard box of pills. The label said "Rat Poison" and bore the name of a Vancouver drug company. A final check by the investigators showed no windows in the building, and the only entrance had been propped shut with a stick from the inside.

The dead man's pockets revealed an English halfpenny, a blank notebook and two handkerchiefs, each marked in the corner "J. Bray."

Since there was nothing further to be learned, the body was ordered removed for post mortem. In view of the box of poison pills, Chief of Police Lister and Dr. Poole believed it was a straight case of suicide.

In the career of every policeman, however, some ominous incident changes the course of a case. The autopsy on the bearded man provided one of these changes. The bearded stranger hadn't taken poison, he had been shot — three times.

When the examining surgeon lifted the scalp, there were three pistol bullets. One was lying flattened under the scalp a quarter of an inch over the right ear. Another had pierced the skull and lodged just above the nose; the third was under the scalp at the top of his head.

Reported Dr. Poole: "The pieces of the bone were drawn into the membrane of the brain by the bullet that penetrated over the nose. One bullet, an inch further back, had not penetrated the brain. These two bullets did not lacerate the brain substance. The one that penetrated to above the nose no doubt caused death."

At the formal inquest three days later, Dr. Poole gave additional evidence that his examination disclosed nothing else likely to have caused the man's death. He was positive the wounds could not have been self-inflicted — there were no powder burns and no weapon was found in the shack.

One of the jurors asked about the box of rat poison pellets. The doctor replied that he didn't think the man had taken poison. "If he had," said Dr. Poole, "it would have shown on the water surface of the stomach. The irritation would have caused a redness."

The coroner's jury brought in a verdict that the unknown man had died at the hands of some person or persons also unknown. Throughout the hearing, however, District Police Chief Lister had had his doubts. Despite the medical evidence, many things puzzled him.

There was, for instance, the piece of wood propping the shack door shut — from the inside. There hadn't been the slightest chance of the murderer leaving except through that door. How, then, could he have propped the door shut from the inside? Another thing that worried Lister was a mark on the dead man's right cheek. It had apparently been caused when he fell against the tree stump which protruded through the floor. If death from bullets occurred with such suddenness that the victim collapsed and hit his face against the stump, where did the murderer stand? On the roof? An examination of the roof exploded this theory.

From the angle of the wounds, Dr. Poole had stated that the deceased might have been shot lying down. If so, had the dead man been knocked down, and then shot? There were no signs of a struggle

In the 1890s this pioneer wagon road — today called Granville Street — connected Vancouver with the north arm of the Fraser River. The McRorie Ranch was about a mile south of where the photo was taken.

in the shack — no bruises or cuts on the dead man's hands and, most important, no bloodstains on the floor. What was the motive for the crime? In fact, getting down to fundamentals, who was "J. Bray?"

Lister was a man who liked puzzling cases and here he certainly had one. Noted for his meticulous planning, he communicated with the head of the force in Victoria, Superintendent F. S. Hussey. He promptly assigned Constable W. R. Atkins, one of his best men, to assist. In addition, Lister added two of his men, Constable J. B. Marquette and Constable Colin S. Campbell.

Under Lister's direction each officer was assigned a phase of the investigation. Fanning out over the Vancouver waterfront, they gleaned every scrap of information about the man with the beard and the bullets in his head.

First enquiry led an investigator to the drug company of Griffiths & McPherson on Cordova Street. The box of rat poison pellets was sold to a bearded man on April 8. The handkerchiefs bearing the name "J. Bray" were another clue. Checking with the Vancouver City Police, the officers found that a J. Bray had been jailed the previous month. However, no charge had been laid. He'd merely been brought in for safe keeping because of a slight head wound which, he said, had been inflicted by two holdup men.

The record showed that four days later Bray had been transferred to a Vancouver hospital. In hospital he told the same story and after a 10-day stay was discharged.

He had given the City Hotel as an address. A check showed that after his discharge from hospital, Bray had gone back there where a trunk and two valises were being held as security for a hotel bill. He'd picked up one of the valises, promising to pay his bill in a day or two.

Checking on Bray's head injury, Constable Atkins found Dr. McAlpine who had examined Bray prior to his admission to the lockup. "They looked suspiciously like bullet wounds," McAlpine said. "But Bray stoutly denied it."

Could it be, Lister wondered, that Bray had been shot in the head and had walked around for weeks? But then, that theory was absurd. A bullet in the brain causes quick death every time.

Continuing the enquiries, Constable Marquette found a man named Morgan who had spoken to Bray on March 20, the day of the alleged holdup and assault. Bray had told Morgan about the incident and said he'd been robbed of $1.75 but the thieves had overlooked $20 in another pocket. Bray went on to state that he had never owned a gun but that "If I had had one, I sure would have used it."

At the City Hotel where Constable Marquette was checking further on Bray's residence, he made a startling discovery. The dead man's statement about never owning a gun was false. The night previous to the holdup he'd been very drunk in the hotel lobby, at one point brandishing a revolver. The manager had taken the gun and $15 cash from him. Both were returned the next morning.

So Bray had had a pistol in his possession the day of his head injury. Further confirmation was the statement of Bray's former roommate who said the dead man always slept with a gun beside him, especially when he had been drinking. The weapon was described as a small "bull dog" type with a short barrel. In their enquiries the police were also establishing another fact: Bray was a very heavy drinker.

Lister and Atkins next took Bray's trunk from the hotel to Provincial Police headquarters. Among the effects was a bloodstained handkerchief, folded in a way that suggested it had been used as a compress. Unfolded, the handkerchief revealed two holes.

Dr. Kirker, a prominent pathologist, identified the holes as having been made by bullets since there were powder burns on one side of the cloth. Then Constable Colin Campbell made an important discovery. He found a cabin occupied by Bray before he had stayed at the City Hotel. It was meagerly furnished, the bed dirty and unmade. Stains on the wall and a large stain on the floor were identified as blood.

Piecing the evidence together, the police concluded that here Bray had first attempted suicide by shooting himself in the head. He miraculously survived. Wrapping a handkerchief around his head to stop the bleeding , he had then shot himself twice through the handkerchief.

Failing in his two suicide attempts, Bray had told a concocted story to the doctor who dressed his wounds, the Vancouver police and the hospital attendants. None realized that he had three bullets in his head — one of them over his nose resulting in pieces of bone in the membrane of his brain.

Next, to complete the case, the dead man's stomach and intestines were examined by Dr. Fagan, Dominion analyst at New Westminster. His examination showed just over a grain of sulphide of arsenic in the stomach. In addition, he found a quantity of masticated wood and even bits of broken glass, one as large as a 25-cent piece.

It was now obvious that on his discharge from the hospital on April 8, Bray was still determined to kill himself. He had purchased the rat poison pellets, picked up his valise from the City Hotel and headed for South Vancouver.

His movements after leaving the City Hotel on April 8 could not be verified, but he had evidently been living in the woods near McRorie's Ranch. The valise was never found, although a reward was offered for its recovery. In all probability he cached it in the bush or destroyed it. It might have contained further proof of his suicide, the weapon he used and possibly further clues about his real identity which was never discovered.

So ended the amazing case of John Bray, the man who lived for a month with three bullets in his head and finally died by poisoning himself.

It began as a potlatch — a traditional Indian gathering to dispense gifts. But after Chief Kamalmuk's wife, Sunbeam, became involved

# Kitwancool Drums Throbbed a War Dance

Among the impressive totem poles in Victoria's Thunderbird Park beside the Provincial Museum is the Kitwancool totem. Carved by the late Indian master craftsman Mungo Martin, it is a duplicate of the original which was raised over a century ago at Kitwancool between the Skeena and the Nass Rivers. This outstanding example of native carving also could be called the $64,000 totem. That is what it cost the infant province of B.C. in 1883 to send troops and ships north to the Skeena where there was fear of a native uprising and a slaughter of the few whites in the area.

Like all totems, the Kitwancool pole tells a story from Kitwancool mythology. The figure at the bottom of the pole is a woman holding a child, her left hand on its head. She is Will-a-daugh, who once married a person of lower social rank whom she met in the bush. He turned out to be a termite in disguise. In due course she gave birth to a baby. Though to all appearances normal, it had an unfortunate trait. At night it changed into a grub and burrowed underground to chew up the cedar houses. Eventually the villagers laid in wait for the destructive intruder. Before it could change back into a child, they killed it.

In her distraction, the mother went down to the seashore (the tribe lived at what is now Prince Rupert). Here she fervently wished that the earth be covered by water and the villagers drowned. By some mistake, although the waters rose, the only one drowned was Will-a-daugh. Nevertheless, the inundation caused the chiefs of the two clans involved, the Wolf and the Frog, to move their people to the Nass River.

But their problems followed them. One day a man who suspected that his wife was being disloyal was out hunting when he heard a ground hog crying "hea-uk, hea-uk." It was a warning about his wife's infidelity. He hurried back to the village where he found his wife with a stranger, whom he promptly killed. Then, looking round, he noticed the stranger's robe, richly adorned with ermine skins. Immediately he recognized that the intruder was the Prince of all Wolves who had impersonated a human.

Late that night the villagers heard a voice wailing from the sky: "Give me back my son." The murdered man's mother was flying

through the darkness in the guise of a giant woodpecker, the symbol at the top of the totem. They tossed the ermine-trimmed robe on a roof to placate her but it did not work. She wanted her son.

She thereupon called a curse on the tribe, and rain fell for weeks. It rained so hard that the village was in danger of being washed away. Again the Chiefs decided to move, this time to the Kitwancool River in the Skeena watershed.

The quiet life they sought still eluded them. In the 1880s white men appeared in their land and disrupted their traditional ways forever. With the whites came diseases to which the Indians were vulnerable because they had no immunity. In 1887, for instance, a terrible measles epidemic struck the tribes. Hundreds were stricken, young and old. Mothers with babies on their backs found a common death on the trail, and in some families every child died. It was a shocking disaster for the tiny world of the tribes in the Upper Skeena River watershed.

One probable reason for the rapid spread of the dread measles was the Indian tradition of potlatching, or gift giving, during which the host gave away mounds of gifts. The Kitwancools held a big one in the spring of 1883 and invited the Kitzegueclas who lived about 40 miles away on the Skeena. Unfortunately, instead of being a friendly gathering the potlatch turned into a near war.

The reason was a grieving, strong-willed Kitzeguecla woman whose Indian name meant Sunbeam. She was married to Kitwancool Chief Kamalmuk, or "Kitwancool Jim" to the whites. Sunbeam, grieving the recent deaths of her two sons during the measles epidemic, had no relish for the drumming, singing and gift-giving which accompanied a potlatch. She felt sure that Neetuh, a Kitzeguecla shaman, or Medicine Man, had put the dread disease on the boys. She talked incessantly to her husband about it, urging him to avenge the deaths in the "eye for an eye" code that the tribesmen observed.

Finally, Kamalmuk could stand no more. Grabbing his rifle he headed down the trail towards Kitzeguecla. On the way he met Neetuh, the shaman, and killed him.

When word of the killing reached Kitwancool, the visiting Kitzegueclas quickly left, vowing vengeance. For days after drums throbbed on the south bank of the Skeena as the Kitzegueclas prepared for war. Into this frenzied scene stepped the Reverend W. H. Pierce, son of a white man and Indian woman. He was a man held in highest regard throughout the north country. Pierce warned the Kitzegueclas to abandon their warlike aims and eventually his reasonable advice prevailed.

Later, Pierce headed for Kitwancool where he tried unsuccessfully to persuade Kamalmuk to surrender to the police. Afterwards he continued to the small community of Hazelton where he reported the killing to the Magistrate. As a consequence, two Provincial Policemen, Bill Washburne and Franklin Green, headed for Kitwancool to arrest Kamalmuk.

When they entered Kamalmuk's cabin he grabbed a gun and slipped through the back door. Washburne followed him while Green

Kitwancool village where Chief Kamalmuk, or Kitwancool Jim, was accidentally killed by B.C. Police Constable Franklin Green.

Below: A shaman trying to heal a sick boy. When the shaman from Kitsegukla was killed by Kitwancool Jim at Sunbeam's insistence, war nearly erupted.

ran through the front door and to the back. There he glimpsed the fleeing Kamalmuk. Washburne pointed his rifle to the sky and fired a warning shot. When Kamalmuk didn't stop, Green knelt and lined him in the sight of his Winchester, intending to wound him.

Unfortunately, the slug caught Kamalmuk between the shoulder blades and he fell dead. Scores of armed tribesmen promptly confronted the lawmen. The two were lucky enough to disengage themselves from a confrontation that could have resulted in their deaths. When they filed their report at Hazelton, it went forward to Victoria with a suggestion that help was needed.

Head of the B.C. Provincial Police was bearded Superintendent H. B. Roycraft, a man of exceptional bravery and considerable experience in the north country. Four years before he and one Constable had faced 300 armed Indians at Hazelton when he not only arrested a Nishka chief called Hatq for murder but also talked the Indians out of retaliation as was their custom. Afterwards he took his prisoner over 600 miles to Victoria where Hatq was hanged.

The Superintendent now had harsh feelings for his trigger-happy Constable Green as undoubtedly did the handful of whites in the Upper Skeena. They all crowded into the Hudson's Bay Company stockade at Hazelton, convinced that an Indian uprising was imminent.

Roycraft suggested to the Attorney-General that he go to Hazelton and quiet things down. The alarming messages from the North, however, carried more weight than the Superintendent's proposal. Finally, the Premier made the decision. The advice of the policeman who knew the region and the Indians was ignored. Nothing less than a full scale military expedition was the answer. The "savages" had to be taught a lesson.

Lying at Esquimalt Harbour was a brand new addition to the Coast's naval strength — the British 1,400-ton steam corvette HMS *Caroline*. Her 1,440 horsepower pushed her along at 10 knots, and her equipment was of the latest — everything from electric lights to Nordenfeldt quick-firing guns.

Superintendent H. B. Roycraft and his few policemen accomplished what politicians had sent an army to do.

Opposite page: "C" Battery of the Royal Canadian Artillery camped by the Skeena River during the threatened uprising.

Below: In 1888 when the outnumbered police and whites feared an Indian attack they erected a 12-feet-high stockade around the Hudson's Bay Company's buildings at Hazelton.

News of the amphibious expedition to the "Skeena War" gripped Victorians with excitement. Eighty men of "C" Battery, Royal Garrison Artillery, were immediately equipped with special campaign uniforms of khaki duck, made locally in record time. On July 16, 1888, to the martial strains of the "The Girl I Left Behind Me," they marched along dusty Esquimalt Road to board the warship.

Every man had a 50-pound pack, a Snider rifle, a bush knife, and a bandoleer with 40 rounds of ammunition. Ahead of them, as supply ship, had gone the slower coastal steamer *Barbara Boscowitz*. She was loaded with 20,000 pounds of food and 18,000 rounds of ammunition. Aboard her was Superintendent Roycraft and 12 B.C. Police Constables.

As the *Caroline* steamed past Victoria's waterfront, practically everybody in town lined the foreshore to wave goodbye, the women in summer dresses twirling parasols.

From past experience, Roycraft felt that Indians at the Skeena mouth would not be inclined to sell or rent any canoes for fear of up-country reprisal. Therefore, when the *Barbara Boscowitz* called at Alert Bay, Roycraft bought six canoes and took them north. When the flotilla arrived off Port Essington, the head of navigation on the Skeena River, "C" Battery was landed at Metlakatla. From there they were supposed to go as far as Kitselas Canyon by canoe then hew a trail to Hazelton — in all 180 miles of mountain wilderness.

Roycraft watched all these preparations with deep misgivings. Finally he talked with Colonel Holmes, "C" Battery's Commanding Officer, and Sir William Wiseman, Captain of the warship. After describing the ruggedness of the country — the Skeena could rise over 15 feet in a night — and the nature of the Indians, he suggested that he and his policeman go on to Hazelton by canoe and talk with them. He was positive that with proper police action there would be no bloodshed and the law would be upheld.

The Army and the Navy agreed and Roycraft left on the rugged upstream journey with his 12 policemen. By prior arrangement he had Magistrate Napoleon Fitzstubbs meet him at Hazelton. Fitzstubbs had previously been in the police force for about 20 years and he and Roycraft had a harmonious relationship — a fortunate circumstance since violence had flared again.

The reason for the eruption was again Sunbeam. After her husband's unfortunate death by police bullet she had returned to her Kitzeguecla tribe. Shortly afterwards she was standing on the south bank of the Skeena when she noticed two Kitwancool braves on the opposite shore and fired two shots at them. Near her, unfortunately, was an important Kitzeguecla shaman, Tobuskis. The impetuous Sunbeam and her mini-war disturbed his concentration and he grabbed a gun. In retaliation he chased Sunbeam's father into a shack and poured seven shots through the door. One of them killed the old man. But instead of ending the shooting, more was to come.

Afterwards Tobuskis went to the river bank and said, in effect, to Sunbeam: "You annoyed me with your shooting, and your father is dead. Now, if you want to shoot me in retaliation, go ahead."

Sunbeam didn't retaliate, but someone else did. Sunbeam's father was the brother of a Kitzeguecla Chief called Morlcken who decided to regain the family honor by killing the shaman. Instead he only wounded him. Then Morlcken sent an Indian called Billy Gamble to Hazelton to tell the police that a wounded murderer awaited their disposal. Before the police arrived Tobuskis was dead, whereupon Morlcken surrendered to the police.

Fitzstubbs and Roycraft now realized that they faced not only a busy legal session but a complicated one. They started by exhuming the body of Kitwancool Jim, victim of Constable Green's bad judgement. With not enough whites in the area to form a jury, Roycraft solved this dilemma by giving letters of dismissal to six of his policemen so that they could function as a coroner's jury. In the best tradition of British justice, they declared that their fellow officer was guilty of murder.

Formally charged, Constable Green was released on $1,000 bail. Next came an inquest on shaman Tobuskis. The jury heard details of how he shot Sunbeam's father and was then wounded by Morlcken, who sent for the police. Justifiable homicide was the verdict and Morlcken went free.

The Skeena War ended not with firing the 18,000 rounds of ammunition carried on the *Barbara Boscowitz* but with a pow-wow. Roycraft and Fitzstubbs made lengthy speeches, to which 13 chiefs representing seven tribes made appropriate replies. In their talks, Roycraft and Fitzstubbs explained the white man's law. The chiefs, repentant, vowed there would be no more trouble.

Afterwards Roycraft reinstated the six policemen who had been discharged to serve as jurors. With their prisoner, Constable Green, they embarked on their 180-mile journey down the rapid-strewn Skeena River. At Metlakatla they told Colonel Holmes that the Skeena War was over. "C" Battery struck their tents and boarded the *Barbara. Boscowitz*, still with 18,000 rounds of ammunition in her hold.

The final chapter of the Skeena trouble was written that November at a special Assize at Nanaimo where ex-Constable Green appeared to answer a charge of murdering Kamalmuk. A jury of Nanaimo tradesmen and miners listened with rapt attention to the incredible story of blood feuds on the Skeena that involved the shooting of a chief by a Provincial Policeman, of the latter's arrest, of shamans — alive and dead — of drums that throbbed a war dance, and of a chief's wife called Sunbeam who started the uproar. To the jury the sequence of events was all very confusing and they acquitted Constable Green.

Today, the slain Kamalmuk is commemorated by the Kitwancool totem in Victoria's Thunderbird Park. It is also a reminder of the days over a century ago when Kitwancool drums throbbed a war dance and politicians spent $64,000 on a military expedition instead of listening to the advice of Police Superintendent H. B. Roycraft.

# Shackled, Starved and Chained

A century ago prisoners weren't pampered. Chained and shackled together, they worked nearly 12 hours a day, usually breaking stones by hand. Their cell was about the size of a cupboard, without light or plumbing.

A familiar sight to residents of Victoria from the late 1850s to the 1890s was that of convicts repairing streets. Although guards were few there was no chance of the prisoners escaping. They were not only chained together but also shackled with leg irons which weighed 14 pounds and were rivetted on. They worked from 6:30 a.m. to 6 p.m. in summer, but were given a reprieve in winter. Hours then were only 8 a.m.

At lower left is a pair of shackles preserved at the Provincial Archives in Victoria.

until dark. They spent the long night in a cell not much bigger than a cupboard, 4 x 8 feet, with no light or plumbing.

Their home for many years was the grim, fortress-like Bastion Square Jail. But it became overcrowded and in 1886 was replaced by the new Hillside Jail. This three-storey building incarcerated 66 male and nine female prisoners. The women's cells were 7 x 9 feet, the men's 6 x 9 feet, still without plumbing. The daily diet was a pint of cornmeal gruel morning and evening; the midday meal a pint of soup, supposedly containing three ounces of meat. Tea, coffee, minus sugar or milk, helped it down. Two days a week fish was served.

The monotony of the diet was relieved only by a punishment schedule that included being handcuffed to the cell bars for hours at a time and, for variety, shoved into solitary confinement on bread and water. There was no attempt at rehabilitation, and even as late as 1897 boy offenders of 10 and 12 labored with hardened criminals.

A main street in Victoria in the late 1860s. The stones in the foreground were originally rocks broken by the chain gang then used to cobblestone the streets. While the prisoners worked they were shackled and chained together.

The 1880s was the era of shackling, when men dragged their way into U.S. courts wearing an "Oregon" boot — a weight fastened to their right leg. B.C. used the British system of leg-irons. They weighed seven pounds each, and in a special "shackling" room were rivetted on when convicts began their sentence, then knocked off with a cold chisel when they were discharged.

Ordinary leg-irons had two long links connected with a small central ring. When out working, the prisoner looped this ring through his waist belt to hold up the irons. Fourteen-pound irons were additional punishment for disciplinary breaches.

It was in this atmosphere that the Federal government in 1876 built the first B.C. penitentiary on the north bank of the Fraser River near New Westminster. Designed to house long-term prisoners, its occupants included U.S. robber Bill Miner who eventually escaped. (See Heritage House Book, *Bill Miner: STAGECOACH AND TRAIN ROBBER.*)

In the late 1880s, A. H. McBridge was Warden, a man utterly unsuited to the job. Worse, he was dominated by a bullying Deputy. He delighted in making the already harsh conditions worse, curtailing the few writing and visiting privileges for months, compounding punishment for the slightest reason, and stealing and selling the inmates' inadequate food. Eventually, a prisoner named O'Connor had the courage — or the desperation — to challenge the Deputy.

O'Connor had been forbidden to write letters or see legal counsel, and received the full range of brutal punishments. One day, pleading his case in the Warden's office and getting nowhere, he jumped through a window. A guard's bullet caught him in the leg and he was quickly back in his cell since there was no hospital.

O'Connor's idea was to be charged with attempted escape so that he could tell his story in a courtroom. For a time it looked as though he would fail because the Deputy wouldn't lay a charge. Finally, he did. O'Connor's counsel, an Irishman called William N. Bole, who was also New Westminster's Police Magistrate, had a difficult time seeing his client. But finally Bole was able to tell the New Westminster Fall Assize in 1885 of the Deputy's cruelty and the harsh conditions.

"Surely," said Mr. Justice McCreight, "this could not have happened. There must be some mistake."

But there was no mistake, and O'Connor summoned guards to confirm his story. One, named Fitzgerald, said O'Connor was "treated like any other prisoner." Then he explained what this treatment meant. One convict called Barry "...has been in solitary confinement, leg-ironed, for the past 19 months."

"Doesn't he get out for exercise?" inquired his Lordship.

"Oh, yes, he gets out," replied the guard, "for 30 minutes a day. On these brief occasions he was handcuffed in addition to being leg-ironed."

Some guards told of special privileges — some prisoners got a bit of cloth for each ankle to stop the chafing. Some unfortunates spent upwards of two years in shackles, in cells 4- x 8-feet square, with no lights or plumbing. Because there was no place to transfer insane prisoners, they stayed in the penitentiary. There were four of them. To enliven O'Connor's existence, the Deputy Warden had one placed each side of him. One was a Chinese who shouted all night; the other, a Negro who screamed all day.

The jail, built for 67, now housed 101. Perhaps the lack of a trans-continental railroad accounted for the fact that the institution hadn't been inspected in seven years. Said Bole in his address to the jury:

"In these menagerie cages men are confined like beasts without exercise or recreation for a year, or a year and a half, loaded with chains. For an attempt to escape this torture O'Connor was shot down like a dog, thrust into solitary confinement and left there 13 months. He made the escape attempt so that he could be brought into court. Now it's proposed to send him back."

Crown Counsel Angus J. McColl replied, with Victorian stuffiness:

"What are we trying to do here? Hold an inquiry on penal methods?" He went on to remind the jury it should be our care not to let such appeals divert our minds from the stern demands of justice. "It's intended that a term of imprisonment should be one of punishment and not of pleasure."

The jury found the prisoner guilty, adding a recommendation for mercy and the suggestion that the penitentiary should be inspected.

Not long afterwards the prison's Roman Catholic chaplain brought about a public inquiry. The chaplain wrote a letter to Mr. Justice Gray of the Supreme Court. Although he was criticized for his action, his letter started an expose of the graft, sadism, and mismanagement in the penitentiary.

The Deputy Warden had to admit that he had "lost track" of 2,000 sides of bacon and 4,000 sacks of flour. Of the 26 guards, 20 hadn't a good word for him. One courageously classified his superior as "the biggest thief in the country."

The public conscience was at last awakened and soon after that there were changes. Leg-irons were discarded, a reformatory for boys was opened in Victoria, and there were innovations such as time off for good conduct. Soon British Columbians began to miss the familiar chain gang on city streets.

Behind it all was the burglar called O'Connor who unwittingly started a reform of B.C.'s prison system. In the Provincial Archives in Victoria his memorial is in a glass case. It is a pair of 14-pound leg-irons.

Mr. Justice Denis Murphy presided at the trial which involved one of B.C.'s most unusual murder cases.

# The Cremation of Sibboo Singh

One of B.C.'s strangest cases of circumstantial evidence, it involved a brutal killing and an innocent family charged with murder.

On March 5, 1914, Matsqui Municipal Constable Jack Cannon had a visitor who identified himself as Mohan Singh, a sawmill worker from Coghlan near Abbotsford. In broken English the turbanned caller told a rambling story about his friend Sibboo Singh. He had suddenly quit his job at the Coghlan mill four months ago and hadn't been heard of since. Mohan felt that Sibboo Singh had met with foul play.

Questioned for details, Mohan related that Sibboo's friend, Rajma Singh, was apparently the last person to see Sibboo. Rajma had been with him on October 29, 1913, when Sibboo left the mill. He waited for him while Sibboo got his $48 pay cheque and casually mentioned to one of the workers that Sibboo might be going back to India. It could have been true, Mohan said, but Sibboo had promised to write within two months. No letter had arrived.

Since then Mohan and some of his fellow workers had met Rajma and asked how Sibboo was getting on. They had noticed a curious contradiction in Rajma's story. To some he said that Sibboo had gone to Nanaimo, to others it was Victoria, and to still another it was Vancouver. Mohan told Cannon that he was concerned about these variations because he had heard that Rajma killed a man in India. Perhaps he had also done away with Sibboo.

Cannon took a description of the missing man, noting that he always wore a salmon-pink turban. Next day he called at the Coghlan mill where he verified that Sibboo had left four months before, and that Rajma was with him. Cannon also learned that Rajma, who hadn't been seen for a week or two, lived alone in a cabin at Aldergrove. His nearest neighbors, a Danish family called Knudsen, lived half a mile away.

Two days after Mohan's visit, Cannon headed for Rajma's isolated cabin. The door was padlocked. The policeman then noticed that there had been some recent clearing on the 10-acre tract. After he'd walked around the cabin trying to peer through the dirt-grimed windows, he went over to inspect the remains of a slashfire. The fire had been out for some weeks, but it had been a hot one. Cannon looked over the ground. There was something strange about the burned, pulverized soil. Someone had tried to cover over one burned patch with fresh soil.

His curiosity whetted, Cannon found a shovel and started to dig. About three feet down he came upon a quantity of discarded tin cans. But, on a hunch, he kept digging. Five feet down he uncovered a piece of pink turban. By now he found himself in a deep hole and, to get out, began digging a side cut. He then uncovered some badly burned boots and a small piece of charred bone.

Deciding he needed expert advice, he drove back to Aldergrove and phoned Dr. Stewart, the Mission coroner. He identified the bone as part of a human right arm. "You'd better go at this carefully," he cautioned Cannon. "Sift all the soil. Bring me everything you find."

Cannon got the other half of the Matsqui police force, Constable Peter Keay, to help him. They unearthed the fragments of a man's suit, some tin trouser buttons, the metal parts of suspenders, shirt buttons and a few more pieces of charred bone. They also took from the scene a coal-oil can with a few drops of coal oil in it.

Back they hurried to Dr. Stewart who now had a further comment: "This is all extremely interesting, but you haven't come up so far with any part of a skull. Better go back and try again."

Next day the two policemen carefully sifted the burned earth of a wider area. They eventually found some rounded pieces of bone, as well as what appeared to be little nuggets of gold. They also found eyelets from a pair of shoes, shoe nails and human teeth.

Dr. Stewart identified the bone as parts of a skull. It seemed that Mohan Singh's suspicions were justified.

Since Rajma Singh's cabin had remained unoccupied, Cannon

began looking for him. The first place he and Keay visited was the Knudsen farm. They were Danes, newcomers to the valley, hardworking and efficient. They knew Rajma pretty well, sometimes inviting him in for a meal. Now and again her four sons went over at night to play cards with him. They said he was a hard worker and fairly intelligent, but they didn't know where he was. Seems he had left the district a week or so before, and they thought he might be working in a mill at Harrison. They had seen another Hindu around his cabin the previous fall, but only for a day or two.

Cannon, the untrained, rule-of-thumb investigator, had done well so far in finding human remains. Now he wondered if Sibboo had a bank account somewhere, maybe some mail waiting for him. Enquiries at Abbotsford were unsuccessful. But at the Mission Bank of Commerce he learned that Sibboo Singh had had a savings account but withdrawn all his money on October 29 the year previous. The bank manager could not remember if Sibboo was accompanied by anyone.

Still checking around Mission, Cannon ran into the C.P.R. station agent who had some surprising information. A week or so before a Hindu and a white woman enquired about the price of a single fare to Edmonton. They then moved to a corner and had a long conversation. The man seemed nervous and excited and eventually they left without buying the ticket.

From the station agent's description, the man was Rajma Singh; the woman, Mrs. Knudsen. Policeman Cannon was puzzled. If Rajma Singh was the murderer, was Mrs. Knudsen helping him to leave? If so, why?

Further enquiries revealed that a week before, Rajma had boarded an eastbound train at Harrison, destination unknown. When Mrs. Knudsen was asked about the ticket, she said that she happened to be in Mission one day and ran into Rajma. He seemed nervous and in trouble. He wanted help in buying a ticket for Edmonton, but didn't have enough money. She hadn't seen him since.

To help find Rajma, Cannon sent out a police bulletin. Quickly came a wire from the Alberta Royal North-West Mounted Police (today's RCMP.) They had Rajma, waiting to be questioned. He'd been found working for a farmer.

Off went Cannon to Alberta to bring back his suspect and lock him up. The Constable obviously favoured the direct approach to questioning a suspect. According to Rajma, he said: "If you don't want to spend the rest of your life in this jail, you'd better tell me what happened to Sibboo."

Rajma said he didn't know anything. The last time he saw Sibboo was in November. He was on his way to Vancouver. A few hours later, however, Rajma said he would like to make a statement.

It was Knudsen who had killed Sibboo, he said, and he'd seen it all. It was about noon, one day in the first week of November. He was walking near a patch of alder between his cabin and Knudsen's when he saw Knudsen and Sibboo quarrelling. Suddenly Knudsen, who was carrying a stick, struck the Hindu three times over the head. Sibboo collapsed. Knudsen went back to sawing some wood nearby. When Rajma reached Sibboo he was shocked to find his friend dead.

"How did you know he was dead?" asked Cannon. "Did you examine him?"

"No. I just knew he was dead."

"Was there any blood on his head?"

"No."

"Were there any marks on him?"

"No."

Knudsen did not seem greatly concerned. "You've killed him," Rajma said he told him.

"He had it coming to him," Knudsen muttered.

Later he saw Knudsen wheeling the dead man in a barrow toward a small unused shed. He also saw him put his hand in the dead man's pocket and pull out a roll of bills. That night, according to Rajma, the Danish farmer set fire to a pile of dead timber on which lay the luckless Sibboo. Two nights later Rajma told Knudsen he was afraid and was going to tell the police. It was then, said Rajma, that Knudsen pulled out a large roll of bills. Peeling off $220, he gave it to him, saying, "Take this and keep quiet."

Cannon couldn't help thinking that $230 was the amount withdrawn from the Mission bank, and wondered why Knudsen had held back only $10.

A day or two later, Rajma continued, he again met Knudsen and said he was still scared.

"Get out of the district ... get out of the country if necessary," counselled Knudsen.

"Where will I go?" asked Rajma, saying that the only part of Canada he knew was the Fraser Valley.

"Go down to the States," replied Knudsen. The next day Rajma and one of the Knudsen boys headed for the border. The U.S. Immigration turned Rajma back, but the boy went through.

After that they decided on the prairies. Mrs. Knudsen went with him to Mission to buy a ticket for Edmonton.

"Did she know about the murder?" asked Cannon.

"Yes, she knew all about it," said Rajma.

Rajma went on to state that he walked the track to Harrison where he worked for a few days in a sawmill, then took a train for Kamloops. After a day he caught another train to Calgary and ended up on a farm.

He spoke of his property at Aldergrove, noting that when he discussed with Knudsen the possibility of leaving, he didn't know what to do about the land. "Sell it," said Knudsen. "Sell it for what you can get."

"But there will be terms to arrange, papers to sign," Rajma pointed out.

"Transfer the title to me and while you're gone I'll make a sale," Knudsen said. "Later you can let me know your address and I'll send you the money."

On that basis, stated Rajma, he transferred the property.

After Rajma signed his statement, Constable Cannon wondered what to do next. He had never experienced a situation like this.

First he had to prove that a murder had been committed and that Sibboo was the victim. He arranged for an inquest. A jury reviewed the pathetic array of buttons and bones that filled 20 envelopes and Rajma told his story. The result was a murder verdict. Knud Knudsen was arrested on a murder charge, his sons Carol and William as accessories after the fact. At the preliminary hearing Knudsen and son, Carol, were committed for trial. The charge against William was dismissed.

There are, fortunately, checks and balances in our judicial system that keep the wheels of justice more or less on the rails. One of these is the Attorney-General's Department. It promptly tossed the whole Knudsen matter into the hands of B.C. Provincial Police Superintendent Colin S. Campbell. As a consequence of their investigation, they realized that the Knudsen family knew nothing of Sibboo's disappearance. The charges were dropped, and Rajma was charged with murdering his friend.

The Knudsens were now Crown witnesses. That fall Mr. Justice Denis Murphy heard the case.

Mrs. Knudsen related that she helped Rajma Singh at the Mission ticket office with no knowledge that she was assisting a possible fugitive. The sons testified that they watched Rajma stoking some big slash fires in early November, that he had said his friend Sibboo had gone back to India, and one night flashed a large roll of bills. Rajma said the money was repayment of a debt by Sibboo before he left, that he'd gone with him to the bank at Mission to get the money. Rajma told the Knudsens that Sibboo had another account in a bank at Cedar Cottage but had left without drawing the money. Rajma wanted to know if they could help him get the funds because Sibboo had said he could also have them.

Rajma's rather weak account of the stick-killing was reviewed — the account of a man killed with a stick and no blood and no marks.

Knudsen described to the court how he came to hold title to Rajma's property. Rajma was in a hurry to leave and asked Knudsen to sell the acreage for him. Knudsen asked how much he wanted and Rajma had replied $500. Knudsen thought he must be in a hurry, for he knew the Hindu had paid $750 for the land, and could have sold it for at least $850.

The five-day trial ended with the jury out for just over an hour. Their verdict was "guilty." Rajma died on New Westminster's gallows on February 6, 1915.

# Cabin Fever— or Perfect Murder?

**"Well, here goes," said the Police Sergeant. Then he began sawing off the old trapper's head.**

Winter, brutally cold and stark white, gripped B.C.'s Peace River Country in mid-December, 1907. But despite the deep freeze, in an isolated trapper's cabin near Pouce Coupe two men stood prepared to perform a bizarre operation.

The beaver cap of one, Staff-Sergeant Kristjan Anderson, bore the buffalo emblem of the Royal North-West Mounted Police (today's RCMP). His companion was Justice of the Peace Calkin. Neither had shed their coats for the temperature inside the fireless cabin almost equalled the -20°F weather outside.

Calkin held the only illumination, a flickering candle that threw eerie shadows on the mud-chinked walls and the grim-featured policeman. He stood poised, handsaw in hand, over the frozen body of a man outstretched on a box. "Well, here goes," said Anderson, and began sawing the cadaver's head off. It was a bloodless operation, for the dead man had been lying in the cabin's ice-house temperature for two weeks.

The circumstances that resulted in George W. Coleman losing his head went back six months to the previous June. It was an era when this B.C. frontier saw an increasing influx of settlers, most via Edmonton, then the end of steel. At Edmonton two of the newcomers, George Stanfield and Frederick Trumper, met the slightly built 60-year-old George Coleman.

Stanfield and Trumper, both bachelors in their thirties, were in Washington when they first heard the call of the north. Stanfield, while a storekeeper for the Oregon, Washington & Idaho Railway, met Trumper who worked in the railway's drafting office. The two became close friends.

Their new companion, Coleman, was also an American who had been all over the Northwest, trapping and prospecting. Trumper and Stanfield, thinking his experience would be useful, took him in as an equal partner. With a team and wagon, they journeyed some 300 miles northwestward into B.C.'s Peace River section. It was late June when they built their 12- x 16-foot log cabin on Pouce Coupe Prairie in preparation for a winter of trapping.

From the start there was a rough division of labor, but soon it was evident that the quiet and scholarly Trumper wasn't exactly a frontiersman. In fact, he could be summarized by the frontier expression: "He had to stand in a washtub before he cut kindling so that he wouldn't injure himself." He frequently mislaid his traps, and when found they were often unbaited or sprung. Although he was a civil en-

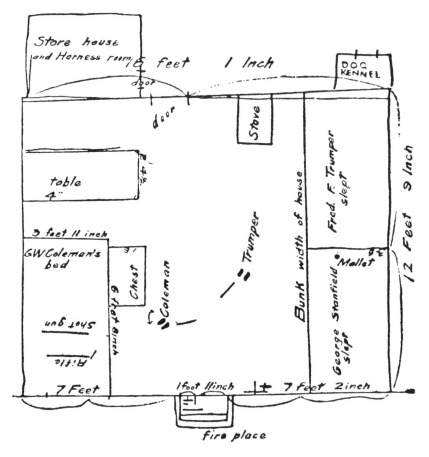

Store house
and Harness room

**Store house**
**and Harness room** 6 feet    1 Inch

door

door

Stove

DOG
KENNEL

12 Feet 9 Inch

table
4"

Fred. F. Trumper slept

Trumper

Bunk    width of house

3 feet 11 inch

G.W. Coleman's
bed

Chest

9'

6 feet 9 inch

Coleman

Trumper

George Stanfield
slept

Mallet

8'

Shot gun

Rifle

7 Feet

1 foot 11 inch    7 feet 2 inch

fire place

Trumper's own sketch of the death
scene which was used at the trial.

The Clinton Courthouse from which Trumper
emerged a free man.

gineer he had no sense of direction. When he missed the trail, which was often, his horse Buck brought him home.

Finally, it was mutually agreed that he would stay home and cook. This chore can be fairly simple if there is a shopping center nearby, but in the isolated wilderness it requires skill. Again he failed, particularly since part of his job was to provide meat by killing game. By contrast, Stanfield quickly adapted to frontier ways and became a fair trapper. Old Coleman, meanwhile, had proved sour and aloof. "I'll cook my own meals from now on in the open fireplace," he told his companions one day, "and you two fellows can cook yours on the stove. And for the future, I'm going to trap with my own traps on my own line."

Most of the original work of building the cabin had been at Coleman's direction for he was an expert with an axe. The fireplace had been his personal triumph. There came a day, however, when its arch collapsed, spilling rocks and clay over the cabin floor. Grumbling and cursing, old Coleman set to work rebuilding it. As he did, Trumper suggested he was doing it the wrong way. "You have to start building it from the haunch," he said, "instead of the keystone."

Coleman, the rule-of-thumb backwoodsman, would have none of his "high falutin' ideas." A few days later the fireplace collapsed again.

By October, prompted by some spirit of perversity, Coleman was getting enjoyment from needling Trumper. On one occasion when Trumper was gazing at a strange bird in a nearby poplar, George took aim at it, the muzzle of the shotgun a foot from the unsuspecting Trumper's ear.

Before he fired, the old fellow looked back at Stanfield leaning in the doorway and gave an anticipatory grimace. Stanfield shook his head in disapproval, but Coleman fired. The deafened Trumper leaped in the air to the derisive cackles of his tormentor.

All this time, Trumper kept a diary. On October he noted, "...cooked beans, cut wood and trimmed my beard." That was the day he also wrote, "Coleman's fireplace fell down."

November 10: "Clear and cold. Water froze six inches overnight. Coleman on a tear today. Northern lights were simply superb last night."

On November 15, after riding 15 miles to Hector Tremblay's place, he wrote: "Had bear meat. Better than beef. Got a dozen letters, two engineering magazines and a cook book."

On November 24 he wrote: "Coleman off for the day. George wrote letters. I finished the washtub made from a 12-inch poplar log. Had boiled spuds, bacon, bread and dried apples for supper."

On November 25, Trumper noted: "Clear and cold all day. George went out over his line to bring in his traps. I started over my line 30 minutes later. Saw two pheasants but didn't get a shot at them. Got back about 3:30 after getting off the trail again .... Found Coleman dead on the floor and George gone to Tremblay's. Chimney caught fire during the evening."

That day George Stanfield had returned to the cabin from his trapline about 3 o'clock in the afternoon. He first noticed that the cabin was extremely warm. Then with a shock he noticed something else — Coleman lying face down, his head in the fireplace.

Rushing over, Stanfield hauled the old man into the room, noticing that he had suffered terrible burns. He hastily doused the charred cloth with a pan of water, then realized that it no longer mattered. Coleman was beyond help. Scattered near the side of the dead man, Stanfield saw a number of bank bills which he collected and placed on the table.

There had been just a couple of charred embers in the fireplace when Stanfield found Coleman, but by the dislodged lumps of clay among the ashes he felt that there must have been a massive fire burning. He examined the woodpile each side of the fireplace — if any had been used, it had been replaced.

Stanfield scribbled a hasty note for his absent partner, Trumper, saying he'd discovered Coleman dead and was heading for Hector Tremblay's Trading Post to report the matter. Leaving the note on the table, he saddled Buck and rode the 15 miles to Hector's, the region's only settler.

Hector sent an Indian with a note to the Royal North-West Mounted Police post at Spirit River, Alberta, 35 miles to the east. (At that time there was no B.C. Provincial Police post in the whole of the Peace River country. In fact the nearest police officer to Pouce Coupe was at Quesnel over 300 roadless miles away.)

Stanfield spent the night with Tremblay, then the pair returned the next morning to the cabin. There they met Trumper who could offer no further details. He'd come in from his trapline to find Coleman lying in the middle of the floor and George's note on the table. While awaiting George's return, he'd dragged the body to the stable and covered it with a blanket.

Finally, after some discussion, the three decided that Coleman must have had a heart attack and fallen into the fire, possibly after piling on more wood than usual. While Stanfield was probably puzzled about how the old man's head had got so deep into the fireplace — only an inch from the back wall — he said nothing.

There being nothing they could do until the police arrived, they took Coleman's remains back to the cabin and put them on a bunk. Nailing the door securely, they all returned to Tremblay's Post.

On December 11 Staff-Sergeant Anderson arrived with Justice of the Peace Calkin and took individual statements. When he finished Stanfield was amazed to learn that Trumper had been arrested.

Apparently, Trumper had stated that he and Coleman had had a heated argument that morning. Finally, Coleman whirled round to grab his loaded rifle from the beam above his bunk. Sensing danger, Trumper reached under Stanfield's bunk and seized the mallet he'd been using to make the wooden washtub. As Coleman attempted to level his gun, Trumper twisted the muzzle to one side. Coleman, trying to duck the uplifted mallet, turned and caught the blow on the back of his head. The old man collapsed in the fireplace. Trumper, in panic, rushed out of doors and for a while wandered around in a daze. When he returned he saw that Coleman's body had been dragged out of the fire, and found Stanfield's note.

The inconsistencies in Trumper's story was the cause of his arrest. For one thing, when Stanfield found the body, both Coleman's rifle and shotgun were in their accustomed place above his bed. Then there was the excessive fire. It was so hot that from Trumper's diary it appeared that the chimney caught fire after Coleman's death.

After Trumper's arrest, the five men visited Coleman's cabin where Anderson and Calkin went carefully over it. The Staff-Sergeant made a rough sketch of the interior, noting the loaded shotgun and rifle above Coleman's bunk. He went through Coleman's letters and cheque book, finally collecting the charred money on the table. Next he searched beneath the bunks and sifted through the ashes in the fireplace, retrieving pieces of Coleman's skull. When he examined the corpse he discovered Coleman had suffered a massive blow on the back of his head.

It was prime evidence, but rather than struggle with the body some 50 miles to Spirit River, Anderson cut off the head and placed it in a bucket lined with straw. Re-wrapping the corpse in blankets, he slung the boardhard remains to a rafter with two ropes. Before he secured the cabin Trumper asked if he could sketch the interior in case he needed it for his defence. Anderson agreed.

Coleman's head was shipped to Edmonton where medical opinion confirmed that a blow with a blunt instrument had caused Coleman's death. Dr. Braithwaite, making the examination, prefixed his report with the statement: "...the head had been taken off with a clean sweep; sawn off at the level of the shoulders."

Coincident with an autopsy, for now Coleman's body had followed his head to Edmonton, came the realization that the killing had happened in British Columbia. There were immediate wires to B.C. Police Superintendent Fred Hussey in Victoria. As a consequence, Staff-Sergeant Anderson and his prisoner were sent to Kamloops, along with the unfortunate Coleman's body and head, each in a separate metal container.

In May 1908, Frederick Trumper's life depended on the decision of a 12-man jury of Cariboo cattlemen, storekeepers and prospectors in a Clinton courthouse. He was defended by Denis Murphy, son of a pioneer Cariboo innkeeper. For this reason, Murphy had a grassroots knowledge of the psychology of trappers, cowpunchers and prospectors — particularly those who lived in isolated cabins where boredom and loneliness could occasionally rouse deadly anger.

There were assumptions and inferences that built up the circumstantial picture of what had happened between Coleman and Trumper in the snowbound Peace River cabin. Finally, however, the Cariboo jury refused to convict on circumstantial evidence.

Fronting the courthouse was Clinton's main street. Frederick Trumper walked onto it a free man.

Opposite the Madden house was Number 2
Fire Hall which helped solve the
22-year-old murder mystery.

# The Case of the Talking Skeleton

**Well, the skeleton didn't really talk. Nevertheless, the quarter-century-old remains revealed a remarkable story.**

The mystery started on an August 1912 afternoon after wreckers had demolished an old frame house on Seymour Street in Vancouver, just opposite No. 2 firehall. They had broken up the concrete walls in preparation for a new office building when a workman uncovered a human skull and leg bone under the earth-floored basement.

Soon Detectives Bob Tisdale and Dick Levis were on the scene. They removed the remaining earth to find a complete skeleton.

Later a police surgeon identified the bones as those of a male, below medium height, between 30 and 40. Levis thought immediately of a man reported missing eight months before. But the doctor shattered this theory by pointing out that the bones had been so long in the ground the death could be stretched to 8 years, or 18 for that matter.

After unsuccessfully checking the records on a variety of missing people, the detectives turned to the ownership of the house. By city tax records they found it had been built in the late 1880s, had been owned by a dozen people, and sheltered at least twice as many tenants who had drifted in and out of Vancouver during boom and bust cycles.

By now the detectives were stymied. Then an unexpected ally

came to their assistance. At this time the *Nicola Valley News*, published in Merritt, got a new editor who decided to liven up the front page by publishing the skeleton story from a Vancouver daily paper. A few days later Nicola Valley resident James Hamilton read it.

Hamilton's memory was jolted by the phrase "...opposite No. 2 Fire Hall on Seymour Street." Over 20 years previously he had boarded with a couple on Seymour Street across from the fire hall. He still remembered their name — Madden. The husband was quiet and hardworking, short in contrast to his large and sporty blonde wife. He remembered, also, that the Maddens had taken in a second boarder named Fletcher. He was a good-looking bachelor who seemed to be attracted to Mrs. Madden — and vice-versa.

Maybe Madden noticed what was going on, for soon after he left. It was a strange departure, not even a goodbye to the neighbors. Months later, came word through Mrs. Madden that he was working in San Francisco. Months later, again through Mrs. Madden, Hamilton learned that her husband had died. As he recalled these events he

A Klondike dance hall girl in the early 1900s. In Dawson City Mrs. Madden also became one of the saloon entertainers, known as the "Big Blonde."

began wondering if Madden had ever gone to San Francisco. Could the bones in the basement be his?

The more he thought, the more suspicious he became. Finally, he wrote to the Vancouver police and later went to see them. With a detective he positively identified the burial place as being the Madden's basement. In addition, his description of Madden matched that of the skeleton, including the fact that Madden wore size 5 shoes.

Only rotting remains of clothing had been found with the skeleton, but they were enough for Hamilton to identify as a type of corduroy that Madden frequently wore. Since there was no sign of violent death, the police concluded that Madden had been poisoned.

Detective-Inspector John Jackson now took up the trail by correspondence to learn that there was no record of Madden's death in San Francisco. In fact, there was no record of his entry into the U.S. On the other hand, local enquiries proved that Madden had not been seen in Vancouver after the spring of 1890.

Probing further, Jackson discovered that in the fall of 1890, Mrs. Madden had gone to Rossland and stayed only long enough to sell some property her husband owned. From there she was traced to Chicago where, it seems, she had been born and raised. She was only there two months when she remarried and, as Mrs. Fletcher, returned to Vancouver with her new husband.

The police then found people who knew the couple. From them it was apparent her second husband matched Hamilton's description of the second boarder. Still following the trail, the police learned that they had lived in several areas of the city until leaving for the Klondike in the rush of 1898.

In Dawson City, the North-West Mounted Police continued the investigation. They quickly found old-timers who remembered the Fletchers. They remembered, too, that soon after their arrival the debonair Fletcher became infatuated with a dance hall girl. He left with her for parts unknown.

Mrs. Fletcher stayed in Dawson, known among the sporting element as "Big Blonde." Finally, alcohol and age diminished her popularity. Shunning society, she then lived a semi-reclusive in a little cabin on the outskirts of Dawson City.

In the early 1900s an observant citizen noticed that there was no smoke from Mrs. Fletcher's chimney and no sign of life around the cabin. Mild interest turned to suspicion and the police were informed. When a Mountie arrived he received no answer to his knock. He tried again, then pushed open the unlocked door.

When his eyes became accustomed to the cabin's gloomy interior, he saw that death had come to Mrs. Fletcher. Not a natural death, though. She had been strangled and the cabin rifled! Some thought the crime might have been inspired by local gossip about the gold she hoarded. Whether or not she had any remains a mystery.

One thing, however, she undoubtedly had was a memory — a memory of a man buried at night in a basement in the heart of Vancouver. Although she kept the secret, the skeleton didn't.

It was only a grey wisp of yarn on a piece of
barbed wire. But because of a brilliant investigation
by Detective Gordon Grant it is remembered as

# The Thread That Became Two Nooses

Every rookie policeman is today aware of the remarkable crime solving potential in the miniscule world of hairs and fibres, and particles of metal, glass, paint and blood, among other things. Under analysis of the microscope, test tube and computer, they have provided clues that have resulted in thousands of convictions for every crime from forgery to murder.

Before the advent of modern science, however, there were often occasions when an astute investigator discovered some minute clue and, without benefit of science, followed it to a successful conclusion. One such case involved an old friend of mine, the late Superintendent Gordon Grant the Vancouver Police's Criminal Investigation Branch. It started just after dark on a mid-April evening in 1921 when a prominent young Vancouver businessman, William F. Salsbury, Jr., was walking along Georgia Street. From a darkened doorway, two young hoodlums suddenly confronted him. One held a gun.

Salsbury, an athlete who was one of Vancouver's top oarsmen, struck at his attackers with his rolled up umbrella. The gun discharged. Salsbury slumped to the sidewalk, a .32 bullet through his heart.

The police were called and Detectives Sinclair, Ricci, Foran and Grant answered the call. Descriptions were vague, but apparently there were two men, youngish, wearing caps, one with an overcoat. After the shooting they dashed across Georgia and turned into Thurlow. In his investigation, Grant spoke to the woman who lived in the corner house. She had been on her porch at the time of the attack, near enough to hear one of the fleeing men say, "Down this way."

At the end of the lawn, one of them fell against a foot-high single strand of barbed wire that kept stray dogs off the newly seeded lawn.

When Grant returned soon after daybreak to check for footprints, he found on the wire a fibre of grey worsted — a mere thread about three inches long. Little did Detective Grant realize, as he put the wisp of thread between the pages of his notebook, that it would grow to the size of a rope. Two ropes, in fact.

As part of the investigation, there was a city-wide manhunt with buses, trains and boats checked, and hobos yanked off freights as far away as Mission. After a week of intensive combing, nothing of importance had been learned. Meanwhile, Grant kept thinking about the wisp of thread from the single-strand fence. It might be the key to the solution.

For a start he instructed the jailer to let him have the pants of every man in custody. Carefully he examined them all. None showed a tear or mark in the weave. "From now on, take the pants from everyone we book," was his instruction.

In the next few weeks Detective Grant examined about 500 pairs of pants. He found nothing suspicious about any of them. Then six weeks after the Salsbury shooting he was passing through the Police Station's charge office when he noticed an elderly secondhand dealer being booked for possession of stolen goods. He knew the old man and his Powell Street store, and he also knew the bespectacled old fraud

Alexander Paulson and Allan Robinson.

occasionally cut a few corners. Apparently, this time he had been found with a bundle of men's suits that weren't quite secondhand. In fact, they had been reported stolen before he'd had a chance to sell them.

Grant, still obsessed with pairs of pants, stopped to listen to his plea of innocence. Then an idea struck him. If the old man had a stock of clothing, he might have some men's suits that were not above suspicion. Why not check?

Grant took the dealer back to his grubby store and began examining the suits. Finally, a grey suit made his search worthwhile — the left leg had a slight tear just below the knee. "Where did you get these?" he asked.

The old man studied the garment, then turned to his much thumbed record book. "Got the name here somewhere," he muttered, turning the pages. "Yeah, here it is. Got them from Frenchy."

"Who's Frenchy?"

"Don't know his other name. Everybody calls him Frenchy."

He described Frenchy as about 25, medium build, a skid road habitue. Now Grant had to find him. With the same persistence that had uncovered a pair of pants from among thousands, he started probing. After a week he uncovered a positive lead.

The Japanese landlord of the Crescent Rooms — who had already been charged with selling liquor to the Indians — told Grant that Frenchy could normally be found around Harry's Place, a sleazy poolroom and speakeasy. Here Grant learned that Frenchy had been away on the prairies for some weeks, but was now back in town. In fact, it was quite probable he would be at Harry's that evening.

Among the evening patrons was Detective Grant, sitting on a bench reading a newspaper. Shortly afterwards someone greeted a newcomer with "Hi! Frenchy!"

A few seconds later, Grant slipped a hand under the newcomer's elbow and steered him to the street. Frenchy gave his name as Alex Paulson and ten minutes later was seated at Cordova Street Police Headquarters.

The chief topic was the suit. It belonged to someone else said Paulson, a fellow called Allan Robinson who had asked him to sell it. Robinson was in town and could be found. As to the Georgia Street shooting, Paulson said he knew nothing. However, Grant sensed a certain nervousness in Frenchy's bearing and decided to detain him. His fingerprints proved that he had a record of armed robbery, breaking and entering. Studying the previous mug shot, Grant noticed that the last time Frenchy posed for the police camera he had a moustache. Now he had none. Was there a reason?

The answer would have to wait. Locating Allan Robinson was now the priority. Within two days he was found in the Silver Rooms.

"Suit?" he said, in answer to Grant's question. "A grey suit? Why that belonged to Paulson, not me."

Now both suspects were in cells, but on different floors. This tactic, as experience had shown, leads to some somber thoughts in the minds of criminal partners. For, despite the old saying about honor among thieves, if the hangman's noose looms each will betray his partner.

Proof was provided the next morning when Paulson said that he was ready to make a statement. He admitted that on the evening of April 12 he and Robinson were at Harry's Place where Robinson suggested going out to "get some money." Robinson had a .32 calibre revolver, while Paulson had a .22.

As they wandered along Hastings Street, a brightly lit drug store drew Robinson's attention. "Let's take it," he suggested. Paulson thought it too dangerous.

Finally, their wandering took them to Georgia Street where Robinson decided that Salsbury, walking alone, was a good victim. Robinson pulled his gun and demanded money. Salsbury struck at him and Robinson fired the fatal shot.

In their hurried flight Paulson tripped over the strand of barbed wire. On Pender Street they slowed to a walk and eventually arrived back at Harry's poolroom. A few minutes later Paulson went to his room and shaved off his moustache, then left his gun with a friend on Carrall Street. When he returned to the poolroom, Robinson was still there. He told Paulson he had ditched his gun and overcoat. After a hurried consultation they decided they'd better not be seen together. They hid for a week, said Paulson, then hitchhiked out of town and ended up in Moose Jaw. They had returned to Vancouver when they felt that the police would have dropped the investigation through lack of any lead.

How wrong their assumption was became evident next day. Robinson was picked out of a lineup by one of the Georgia Street witnesses. Then Grant found the man with whom Paulson had left his gun. He in turn led to Kam Dale who had recently been discharged from Oakalla Prison. He remembered Paulson and Robinson in Harry's Place the night of the holdup and that they went out for an hour or so, returning about 9:30. Robinson told Dale he'd shot a man on Georgia Street. It was Dale who had then advised Paulson to shave off his moustache.

The pair came up at the October Assize before Justice F. B. Gregory. In an attempt to save himself, Paulson voluntarily gave evidence for the Crown. Judge Gregory was ready for this ploy by warning him to give his evidence "fairly and frankly, honestly and truthfully."

Paulson obviously did not know what "honestly and truthfully" meant. He claimed he didn't have a gun on the murder night. In fact had never owned a gun. In rebuttal his friend from Carrall Street identified Paulson and his gun. In addition, Kam Dale said it was stuck inside Paulson's belt when he left Harry's Place.

Both were convicted and sentenced to death. Robinson appealed and was granted a new trial.

In April 1922, twelve months after the murder, Robinson appeared before Judge Denis Murphy, defended by J. W. de B. Farris and Gordon Sloan. There was no doubt that he had an adequate defense. Both would become Chief Justices of British Columbia.

Again the verdict was guilty. That summer Paulson and Robinson appeared before a hangman at Oakalla.

The tenacious Detective Grant made his name famous in other cases, eventually retiring as Superintendent. Although to the young men in the Department he was Superintendent Grant, to old-timers he was the man who fashioned two nooses from a wisp of worsted thread.

Part of the Chinese section of Victoria in the days of Peach Blossom.

Young and beautiful Peach Blossom felt that
her assets would be worth more in Seattle
or San Francisco than in Victoria. Unfortunately
her quest led not to riches but to

# Midnight Death
# on a Lonely Island

Some 100 years ago, late on a March afternoon, a metal box sank to the
bottom in Nanaimo's harbor. In it was about $1,500 in cash and jewelry worth probably the same. It is likely still there.

How that box came to be dropped in the water is part of an extraordinary tale of human vanity and greed. It involved not only a kidnapping, but the murder of a beautiful Chinese girl on a lonely island.

Perhaps, at the start, it's as well to understand that a century ago
it was fairly common for certain members of Victoria's almost womanless Chinese men to buy and sell women. They ranged in age from 13
to 30, were smuggled from China by various subterfuges, and were
usually deceived about the purpose of the trip by some elderly female
procurer. Many came as wives or daughters of passengers, to be
gathered up on arrival. Under another successful scheme they were
brought in as the all-women Chinese theatre group. Apparently immigration officials had never heard that women did not belong to
theatrical groups — at least not then.

Bought from poverty-stricken parents in China for about $250, the
girls on arrival in Victoria sold for $1,200 to $1,500. Most, especially
the very young ones, had a miserable existence. They lived like
prisoners in dingy tenement back rooms, sometimes never going outdoors for months at a time. The better looking girls were frequently
passed from owner to owner at increasing prices, one of them occasionally gaining status as a sort of favored concubine. In this case,
the girl usually realized that she had a value and extracted jewelry and
other wealth from her "protectors."

One of these girls was 19-year-old Lee Guay. For a cash consideration she had come under the roof of Wong Duck Chun, an elderly but
wealthy Victoria merchant. Affable and urbane, Wong obviously felt
his wealth entitled him to such an elegant household ornament. In admiration of her beauty, he dubbed her "Peach Blossom." Soon he was
lavishing her with fine silks and surprising her with jewelry.

Peach Blossom, instead of being cloistered as the majority of other
girls were, came and went as she pleased. Whether she tripped along
crowded Cormorant Street or climbed into a hired hack for an afternoon drive, the lovely Lee Guay garnered admiring glances. And it
pleased old Wong to see her go out, a living advertisement to his
wealth and importance.

As time went on, however, Lee began to think about her future.
Perhaps it was as the folk song says: "Better a young man with an apple

in his hand, than an old man with a hundred acres of land."

In any event, there recurred the thought that, before her petals wilted, she might be accorded even greater favors by a wealthy but younger protector in Seattle, Portland or San Francisco. Perhaps she voiced her thoughts to someone, for ready ears heard them. They belonged to Ah Sam and Ah Fat, inseparable companions who hung around Theatre Alley and the gambling houses. Unlike their hard-working countrymen, they lived by their wits. Sam, short and thick-set, was a slow thinker; Fat, by contrast, was lean, calculating and emotionless.

On an afternoon in early February 1887, just as a white-robed funeral procession with its clangor of gongs and firecrackers passed along Cormorant Street, the pair intercepted Peach Blossom and invited her to a vacant doorway to listen to an important proposition. Was it true that she wanted to slip away from old Wong and get to Seattle? If so, they had a plan and the means: a hack to the waterfront and small sloop to Puget Sound. The cost, a mere $50.

As interest flickered in the girl's dark almond eyes, the worldly Ah Fat offered a suggestion. As she would have to make a good impression on Seattle's wealthy young merchants, it might be advisable to wear her jewelry. In fact, she should wear all her jewelry. Charm and appearance being Peach Blossom's main asset, she thought it a good idea.

Finally the pair asked about money. Could she raise the fare? It was said in a tone that hinted that old Wong perhaps drew the line at dispensing cash. With a little smile, Peach Blossom assured them that the fare was no obstacle. Just in the past week Wong had supplied her with a duplicate key to his strong box so that she could keep her jewelry safe.

Next afternoon, Lee Guay, clothed in her best and wearing her expensive bracelets and earrings, her mass of gleaming black hair spiked with gold inlaid combs, left for a rendezvous at Cormorant and Government Streets. Round her shoulders she wore a fur-trimmed cloak against the February chill. At the corner she paused for a moment, then stepped into a covered hack and was gone.

When Wong Duck Chun discovered her absence he anxiously enquired around the neighborhood. No one could help him. Night passed, and still no Peach Blossom. Early next morning he was at the police station telling the desk Sergeant in pidgin English that his "wife" had been kidnapped. Wong left $50 in cash as a reward for information.

One question the police asked Wong sent him hurrying home to check his safe. He discovered that not only had the jewelry gone but also about $1,500 in cash. Although upset, the indulgent old man refused to believe that his Peach Blossom had deliberately robbed him. She must have been prevailed upon by the person who had enticed her away.

The police circulated a description of the missing beauty but the following weeks brought no clue. No one seemed to have noticed her getting into the hack, and because of the passing funeral, no one had observed her conversation with two men or noted the absence of Ah Sam and Ah Fat.

Finally, after six weeks of silence, Wong decided to investigate himself. First, he explored the Saanich Peninsula, questioning Chinese truck farmers. Next, with fisherman Lee Look he explored Sidney shoreline in Look's small sloop, through Satellite Channel and up to Cowichan Bay. It was ominous territory to Wong, with few white farmers but plenty of Indians who were not exactly peaceful. They had recently murdered Crofton farmers Jim Miller and Bill Dring in their homestead cabin (See *B.C. Provincial Police Stories — Volume One*), and up the coast the Indians who murdered the crew of the schooner *Seabird* had just been arrested.

Thoughts of Peach Blossom, however, caused Wong to ignore these possible dangers. Finally, at a big Indian camp at the head of Cowichan Bay he got his first lead. One of the tribesmen had heard from another passing brave of two Chinese and a Chinese girl seen on a white sloop near Kuper Island.

At Kuper, Wong and Look got confirmation of the story. The uncommunicative Chinese trio, said the Indians, had camped five days on the beach and bought some eggs. They had left in the dark but nobody knew where. Look guessed north. At Chemainus, Wong gave two Indians $5 to scout Nanaimo Harbor. If the white sloop was there, $15 awaited them. They returned with confirmation that the sloop was there.

Wong and his friend headed northward. As they moved into the harbor they saw the small white sailboat anchored near Vancouver Coal Company's wharf. They drifted alongside. From the sloop's cockpit Ah Sam and Ah Fat regarded the newcomers suspiciously. Although Wong wasn't sure they had anything to do with Peach Blossom's disappearance, his first words were: "What have you done with Lee Guay?"

"We brought her up here so she could take a boat to Seattle," said Ah Fat, Wong's forthright question catching him by surprise.

"What boat?" said Wong coldly. "What was its name?"

"Can't remember," replied Fat.

"Who sold her the ticket?" pressed the old man.

"She didn't have a ticket," came the reply. "We smuggled her onto a collier."

Wong called them liars. At the old man's hostility Ah Fat admitted, with a smile, that the story wasn't quite true. The girl was safe on one of the nearby islands, he said, and he offered to take Wong to her. Wong sensed danger and spoke in a low tone to Lee Look. They moved over to the boat landing and tied up.

Half an hour later Wong was telling his story to Provincial Police Chief Stewart. Soon Constables Sam Drake and Dave Stephenson were pulling across the harbor to the sloop. As they got near, Drake saw Ah Fat lean over and drop into the water what looked like a box.

Although they found nothing of interest on the boat, they brought the pair back to the lockup. Both men insisted that they had brought the girl to Nanaimo and put her on a collier bound for Seattle.

While the police investigated, Wong approached Stewart with a suggestion. He said he had a good friend in Victoria, Ah Wing, who doubled as police interpreter and pawnbroker. He would like to bring him to Nanaimo to talk to the prisoners. Stewart knew there were possible aspects of the suggestion that lay deep in some Chinese brotherhood, but he agreed.

When Ah Wing arrived he asked if he could speak to Ah Sam alone. At the end of half an hour he had a story for Stewart. He had felt Ah Sam was the weak link and so it had proved. Without promise of immunity Ah Sam confessed.

The glamorous Peach Blossom, said Sam, had been murdered in her sleep by Ah Fat as she lay on the beach at the south end of Narrow Island (now Wallace Island). Ah Sam said the killing took place about a month ago. He awoke around midnight to see Ah Fat creep upon the sleeping girl and club her to death. Then he took her jewelry and her money. It was the jewelry and money that were dropped overboard in Nanaimo Harbor.

Next day, on the chartered steamer *Saturna*, Captain Jager with Policemen Drake and Stephenson, Ah Sam and Wong crossed to Narrow Island. They found the charred remains of a camp fire on the beach in a little cove. Nearby was a woman's gold inlaid comb which Wong identified, a bloodstained arbutus wood club, and two keys, one from Wong's strongbox.

The morning after the murder, Ah Sam told the police, they had weighted the body with a large rock and dumped it in the bay. For two days, until the boat was needed for another charter, the police dragged unceasingly.

"Keep at it," was Chief Stewart's injunction after examining the exhibits.

So the quartet returned to Narrow Island, this time in a large canoe paddled by four Indian prisoners. Again they began dragging — a frustrating job because of the seabed's rocky bottom. Finally, in late afternoon of the second day they snagged something that wasn't rock. Although heavy, it slowly yielded.

Carefully the police hauled their catch to the surface and towed it to the beach. In the failing light of that evening in early April, old Wong Duck Chun identified Peach Blossom. Her skull had been fractured by repeated blows of the wooden club, and the lovely face that was to have been Peach Blossom's fortune ceased to exist. One of the Indians muttered something in Chinook. Stephenson nodded, confirming the Indians remark that there were a lot of miniature sharks called dog fish in the bay.

Afterward the police interviewed the Indians who had seen the girl with her abductors. That autumn the whole story was pieced together before Justice Sir Matthew Baillie Begbie and a Victoria jury. Ah Sam and Ah Fat, found guilty, were sentenced to death.

For three plugs of tobacco, a $5 bill and a broken
revolver the old Chinese miner was murdered. But to his
killers these meager possessions became

# Sat Chew's Revenge

It was the first week in September 1908 when Big Louie, an Alkali Lake
brave, started repairing his fishing station on the Fraser River a few
miles north of Dog Creek in the Cariboo. As his people had done for
thousands of years, he was rigging a rough staging above the rocks
and as the sockeye salmon hurtled up the foaming rapid like silver
missiles, Louie's big dip net would intercept them. Trouble was, he
needed one more plank for his shaky platform — and there wasn't one
for miles. Then he thought of an abandoned Chinese miner's cabin a
few hundred feet away. Although there was a padlock on the door,
with a pick lying nearby he quickly yanked the hasp from the weather-
beaten doorpost.

The door was stiff and creaked as he pushed it open to view the
dingy interior. As his eyes grew accustomed to the gloom, he noticed
he wasn't alone. On the floor, more skeleton than corpse, lay the
remains of a man. The startled Indian took a closer look and noticed
the clothing had almost rotted away. With the pick he cautiously poked
the grisly remains. As he did so some of the bones fell apart.

Hastily Louie left, closing the door behind him and replacing the

Joe Place's Hotel and Store at Dog Creek. Here Ah
Chew made the few purchases that helped
convict his killers.

hasp. At the river he told his wife of the discovery, then rode to Dog Creek with the news. Here he told Ah Hing, the Chinese hotel cook. Hing then told his friend, Ah How, who worked for rancher Malcolm Meason.

Next day the two Chinese visited the cabin and satisfied themselves that the dead man was their friend, Sat Chew. Believing that he had died of natural causes, they decided to use a small tin trunk that was in the cabin as a coffin. When they lifted the almost skeletonized figure and doubled it over in the trunk its head fell off. They put it on top of the body and closed the lid.

With the last of Sat Chew in the trunk, the pair rummaged the sparsely furnished cabin, looking for anything of value that they could take care of, but found nothing. Somehow they didn't like to bury the trunk for Ah How felt that possibly the government might want to know about Sat Chew's death. Replacing the staple on the door, they went back to Dog Creek where Ah How told the story to his boss, Meason.

First thing that puzzled Meason was the padlocked cabin. How could the man inside padlock the door on the outside? He decided to investigate and with Chief Joe Bacon of the Alkali Lake Band, rode to the cabin. Inside, Meason looked into the trunk. Certainly seemed to be old Sat Chew, and he'd been dead a long time. Gingerly lifting out the bones, Meason made a discovery. The ribs weren't equal in number — the two right bottom ones were broken off near the spine.

Meason again thought about the padlocked door. Could it be murder? They returned to Dog Creek and sent word to Constable Jack McMillan at Clinton on the Cariboo Wagon Road. Telegraph messages soon brought to the scene McMillan's District Chief, Joe Burr from Ashcroft, Coroner Casper Phair from Lillooet, and Dr. Cecil Boyd from 150 Mile House. Along with Joe Bacon and some Chinese, the group finally reached the lonely Fraser River cabin.

First came identification, although there was no doubt that the remains were Sat Chew. He was a 65-year-old Chinese who had panned gold along the Fraser for 17 years, never making more than bare groceries.

Big Louie described how he found the body lying on its side, one hand up to the face, between the door and a cot. Next Dr. Boyd had the unpleasant job of reconstructing the remains. As he draped the rotting garments round the skeleton he pointed out holes in the clothing "not made by maggots or moths, but by bullets or a sharp instrument."

There were no signs of powder burns around the holes, but inside there was extensive staining that could have been blood. One of the holes he pointed out was level with the lowest two right ribs, both of which were fractured, with pieces missing at the seat of the fracture. There were no injuries to the skull, he reported, and the deceased must have been dead about six months, maybe longer.

Meanwhile Burr, prowling the cabin, spotted a clean hole in the middle of a rice mat hung on the wall behind the bed. Pulling down the mat he probed with a penknife in the hardened mud that plastered the logs. Finally, a bullet fell to the floor. It was slightly deformed, three grease grooves, or canelures, at its base identified it as a .44. Coroner Phair held an inquest in the cabin, the verdict that Sat Chew had been murdered by a person or persons unknown.

Burr and McMillan then tried to learn something about the murdered man's activities. Genial Joe Place, known far and wide as Dog Creek's postmaster, hotel and storekeeper, was able to help them. He said Sat Chew was last in his store about five months before, around the beginning of April. He bought some rice, flour and lard, as well as three plugs of T & B tobacco. They came three plugs to the pound, 35 cents each, or three for a dollar. Old Chew took the pound bargain. He paid with half an ounce of gold amalgam, and got back a $5 bill and some silver — maybe a dime and a nickel.

Next they interviewed Big Louie who had discovered Chew's body. He swore he hadn't touched anything in the cabin, except to give the corpse a poke with the pick before hastening away. He had looked the ground over for tracks before he left, but saw none.

The two Chinese who put Sat Chew's body in the trunk had seen nothing of value in the cabin — no money, no plug tobacco. Checking with the postmaster, the police were told that Sat Chew never sent mail or money orders. Could he have amassed a little treasure of gold that spurred somebody to murder him? Doubtful, was the Dog Creek opinion. Old Chew made just enough for bare necessities. Since he apparently had no enemies, the question was: Who had stayed with him last, or camped near his cabin the previous spring?

One person who camped near him in the early spring was Hazelton's well known packtrain operator, Cataline, accompanied by his assistant, Ah Fook. The police, however, knew that Cataline was a legendary figure throughout Interior B.C. and an unlikely subject for suspicion. Another name that surfaced was Dave Wiggins, who sometimes helped Cataline. It was proved, however, that he'd been at Sheep Creek in the Chilcotin for over a year.

During this time Chief Bacon rode into Dog Creek with something of interest. The week before in his wagon he was three miles from the Alkali Lake Rancherie when his wife saw something on the side of the road. It was a rusty revolver. Chief Bacon took it into Alkali Lake, asking his band if anyone had dropped it. But as no one claimed it, he'd brought it to Dog Creek.

As Joe Burr handled the revolver, hotel cook Ah Hing bustled forward.

"That belong to Sat Chew," he said decisively. "I live with him once. I remember that gun. Him got broken hammer, won't fire."

Sure enough, the firing pin was missing.

The weeks rolled by with Burr still pursuing his enquiries. In early December, the Cariboo deep in winter's grip, Burr uncovered the first significant clue. It was linked with Sat Chew's gun. Whoever had stolen it, and dropped it, must have been heading for the Alkali Lake community. There Burr picked up a story that early in April a big gathering of Indians had indulged in a session of "la hal," the great Indian gambling game. Of the participants, two especially interested

Burr. One was an Indian named Basil who had wagered his .44 rifle and lost it, then a $5 bill, and lost that too. A .44 and a $5 bill! Sat Chew had been killed with a .44 caliber bullet — and his $5 was missing. Even more suspicious was that Basil was accompanied by his pal Louie who had wagered three plugs of T & B tobacco.

It was a lead that Burr and McMillan quickly followed. McMillan arrested Basil at Dog Creek Reserve, while Burr found Louie (no relation to Big Louie who had discovered Sat Chew's remains) between Dog Creek and Canoe Creek at Salt John's place. On the way back, Burr

Ashcroft in the early 1900s, and District Police Chief Joe Burr. Here murder suspect Basil blamed his partner for the killing.

retrieved Basil's .44 rifle which by this time had got into the hands of Andy Brown at Dog Creek.

While McMillan locked up Louie at Clinton, Burr took Basil to Ashcroft. Louie soon decided he wanted to make a statement. It was Basil, he said, who one day in early April thought of killing the Chinese. Saddling their horses, Basil got his .44 rifle. At Sat Chew's cabin Basil told the old man that Ah Fook (Cataline's helper) had asked him to search for a lost horse. Both Indians were in the shack, talking briefly to Sat Chew, then turned and went out. Basil picked up his rifle which was leaning against the outside wall. As Sat Chew said good night, Basil shot him.

Sat Chew fled inside, slamming the door. Louie stated that he ran off, but Basil stood listening for a minute, then beckoned him back. Re-entering the cabin, they found the Chinese sitting on the bed. Basil aimed at him again but missed.

They searched for money but only found a purse with a $5 bill. Basil took the money, then gave Louie three plugs of tobacco and the victim's broken revolver.

They found a padlock in a box, the key to it in Sat Chew's pocket. With the key in his hand, Basil rolled the now dead man off the bed. Then after padlocking the door, he threw away the key. They rode back to Alkali Lake Reserve and played la hal, Basil losing his rifle to Joseph, and the $5 bill to someone else. He lost his three plugs of tobacco to Johnny Squenegan. A day or two after that, Louie concluded, he missed the stolen revolver, and decided he had dropped it somewhere.

But if Louie had a story, so did Basil. That same week he gave his version to Burr at Ashcroft. It was essentially the same as Louie's — with one difference. Basil insisted that Louie had thought of the idea of killing Sat Chew and was the one who fired the shots. Sensing that a hangman's noose could be their fate, each partner energetically blamed the other.

There was a preliminary hearing at Clinton in January 1909. Both men would have appeared at the Clinton Spring Assize but for a distraction. One night Louie's cell was found with the bars cut and Louie gone on a fast horse left handy to the jail.

It was six months before police found him, and autumn before the pair came up before Judge Aulay Morrison, with Jim Murphy defending them. Furiously Murphy battled to prevent the two confessions from being presented as evidence. He was unsuccessful, but did create sufficient doubt to prevent the jury agreeing. The two Indians went back to jail to await the next Assize.

In May 1910, 25 months after the cold-blooded killing, the pair came up before Mr. Justice F. B. Gregory. This time they were not so fortunate. The jury found them guilty.

As meager as Sat Chew's possessions had been, they were plentiful enough to bring him revenge. On July 20, 1910, Basil and Louie mounted the scaffold in the Kamloops jail yard.

Among the unsolved cases in
B.C. Provincial Police files is the

# Mystery of the Tahsis Twins

Harvey and Horace Watters were twin brothers, prospectors who in the early 1900s were known up and down B.C.'s jagged coast. They spent their summers on the streams which cascaded down from the mountains and their winters in Victoria. Bachelors, they were inseparable and, perhaps because they were twins, remarkably tolerant of each other's shortcomings. In fact, so indissolubly were their lives connected that Harvey once remarked: "When Horace dies, I think I'll die too."

The statement would prove strangely prophetic.

One special characteristic the twins shared was booze. But even after over indulging they were genial and good tempered, not only with each other but with those around them. Horace was the thrifty one, with a small bank account in Victoria and income from rented houses. Harvey, by contrast, was the model for the saying, "Easy come, easy go."

In March 1908, following their yearly pattern, they collected their gear and set out for the West Coast of Vancouver Island. As in the past few seasons they would hunt for their pot of gold at Tahsis Inlet, a 20-mile-long fiord that branches in from Nootka.

The twins travelled up on the old *Tees* and got off at Clayoquot. On the way up they had absorbed generous quantities of Scotch and at Clayoquot took advantage of the economy size. They bought a gallon jug since in those days saloon keepers obligingly sold from the barrel, provided the customer paid for the container or brought his own.

Their spiritual needs provided for, the Watters brothers rented a double-ended sealing boat. Harvey paid for it from a fairly big roll and

Until beset by tragedy, the Tahsis Twins annually prospected the rugged fiords that pierce inland from Nootka Sound.

the pair set out for Tahsis. Near Tsow-win Narrows, about 12 miles up, they pulled ashore to camp in a deserted cabin belonging to an Indian. Their own cabin was about a mile farther but it had been crushed by a falling tree.

The only person who saw or spoke to them when they hauled their boat high on the rocky foreshore was Old Scooter, an Indian with a reputation for being extremely honest. He said later that one of the twins staggered slightly when he walked, while the other was despondent, suffering apparently from a violent hangover.

Two months later Scooter passed in his canoe and decided to visit the pair. To his surprise, the place was deserted. As he looked around it was apparent they had been absent quite a while. It appeared, in fact, that they had not spent much time in the place after they landed. Though their bed rolls had been used, then rolled and stacked against the wall, their cooking pot and frypan hadn't been unpacked. In addition, their food was mouldy and the gallon jug of whiskey still nearly full. For safety, Scooter put the bed rolls in the rafters. Then he picked up what he thought most valuable — two small cases and a .45-90 Winchester rifle, and took them to the Catholic priest at Nootka. In his slow Nootkan voice he said that he felt the white men hadn't been around for some time and it was strange.

The priest, knowing Scooter's reputation for truthfulness, contacted Provincial Constable Angus McLeod at Clayoquot. When McLeod arrived he took Scooter as a guide. He examined the cabin and the brothers' sealing boat hauled up on the rocks, oars, rowlocks and sail intact. The vessel was full of water, understandable considering that annual rainfall in the region is some 20 times more than at Kamloops in Interior B.C.

McLeod next circled out from the cabin. Nine hundred feet away, where a vagrant williwaw had felled a little clearing, he discovered the body of a man. He was lying on his back and had been dead some time. At first glance, McLeod thought he had been struck by a falling tree, but rejected this idea when he noticed that the man hugged a shotgun, one hand on top of the barrel, the other underneath. Constable McLeod examined the rusty weapon and believed that one barrel had been fired because a weather-beaten empty cartridge was lying beside the body. Possible suicide was his thought, though he couldn't see any marks of a shotgun charge around the man's head. He could have been mistaken, however, since the body was in an advanced state of decomposition. McLeod searched the clothing but found no identification and no money. All that the body offered was a watch and chain, which McLeod pocketed. Then he took a photo of the corpse, something of an innovation because cameras were not in general use in police investigations. Afterwards he dug a shallow grave and buried the remains.

When District Chief C. A. "Gus" Cox at Alberni received McLeod's report, however, he promptly headed for Clayoquot, picked up McLeod, then went on to Nootka. He appraised the rifle and suitcases, which offered no clue, gave the cabin at Tsow-win a second examination, then exhumed the body and took it to Victoria for an inquest.

About this time Cox realized that the dead man was one of the Watters brothers. But which one? And where was the missing twin? The first problem, that of identification, was soon solved. Rod McKinnon, a former logger employed on the *Tees*, had known the Watters brothers for about 15 years. He noticed them travel up on the *Tees* and get off at Clayoquot. Finally, he identified the watch and chain as belonging to Horace Watters. He was positive because 21 months before he had given it to him.

So Horace was the dead man. But how did he die?

In Victoria a new doctor, Walter Bapty, had joined the city's health department. He was a man with a flair for solving medical puzzles. But after a thorough examination of the remains, even Dr. Bapty was somewhat undecided. Except for the head where a section about six inches square from the right rear was missing, all bones were present and uninjured. Constable McLeod had missed the broken skull because the head was turned to the right and resting on the ground, and the cavity filled with moss. Whether the piece was missing before or after death, Bapty couldn't say. But from its position and the appearance of the cavity, he doubted if it was from a shotgun.

With the mystery deepening, the inquest was adjourned so that Cox and McLeod could again visit Tahsis Inlet. This time they took three experienced bushmen from Clayoquot. Cox, searching where the body was found, finally discovered in the short thick undergrowth the missing piece of the dead man's skull. It was intact, seeming to dispose of the shotgun-suicide theory. But how did a piece of Horace Watter's skull fall out?

Methodically the party searched the shoreline for miles in each direction. Half a mile from the cabin a river barred their way, and Cox wondered whether Harvey had drowned attempting to cross it. Though now a temperate stream, it would have been in full flood in March.

Halfway between the river and the place where Horace's body was found one of the searchers picked up a man's felt hat. It bore the initials HW. But which one? Horace or Harvey? More puzzling still were holes in the crown that might have been caused by birdshot.

Then arrived another fairly shrewed observer — Indian Agent A. W. Neill. To him, District Chief Cox wondered if Indians might be responsible. Neill shook his head. He pointed out that the only Indians near the two white men when they landed were Old Scooter, another man who was badly crippled and Stick Jim, who had his wife with him. The first two could be discounted, and if Stick Jim had been affronted by something the whites had said, or did, he wouldn't have attacked them alone. He would have got help, and it would have taken a week or two. In addition, if they had been responsible for any violence they would have quietly vanished. Instead, Old Scooter, although he did not know there was a dead man nearby, interested himself in looking after their effects. Another point was the whiskey that had remained. Finally, there was the boat. Had the Indians killed either or both of the whites it would have allowed a fast escape.

For that matter, reasoned Neill, wouldn't Harvey have used it if he had killed his brother and wanted to flee? It was the logical way to depart. Behind the cabin was impenetrable bush that quickly became a steep mountainside. Furthermore, if Harvey were responsible, would he have left his food, bedroll and rifle in the cabin? If the gun were his, then he had no thought of danger when he left it there.

Cox wondered whether someone at Clayoquot, seeing Harvey pay for the boat rental from a roll of bills, had decided to rob him. Experience then reminded him that if an Indian were involved, most certainly there would have been some spending. There had been none. In addition, there were no strangers around, white or Indian. The Indian cabins up the inlet were all deserted and would have been until the fall fishing season.

It was suggested that Horace's skull injury might have resulted from a falling tree, but this theory was rejected by those who knew the brothers. They were too experienced to be hit by falling trees.

When the inquest resumed at Victoria a third brother, Dr. Watters from California, as well as G. B. Garrard of Victoria who knew the twins well, testified that drunk or sober, they never quarrelled. The jury finally concluded that so far as Horace Watters was concerned "the manner in which he came to his death is as yet unknown."

The jury's summation also could have applied to Harvey. Could the answer to the mystery be that Horace was somehow killed accidently in the little clearing near the cabin? Could Harvey have then given truth to his statement: "When Horace dies, I think I'll die too!"

The mystery remains.

# The Killers
# Who Hanged Each Other

**After the evidence was presented, Judge Morrison remarked to the jury: "It has been a ghastly struggle between these two men the last three days ... a struggle to death."**

During the 92 years that the B.C. Provincial Police were in existence they maintained law and order throughout the province with the exception of several large cities such as Victoria and Vancouver which had their own police forces. Like policemen everywhere, these city officers never knew when they would be suddenly confronted with men who would kill to save themselves.

Constable James Archibald, murdered on duty in May 1913.

Detective Dick Levis who tracked down the killers. Three years later Levis was murdered by a drug addict.

Such was the fate of Constable James Archibald and Detective Dick Levis. The background was given to me by the late R. L. "Pat" Maitland who became B.C.'s Attorney-General. At the time, however, he was a young lawyer, his first case defending one of the killers.

The story began in the early morning of May 28, 1913, when Constable James Archibald failed to ring in on schedule to Police Despatcher Sergeant J. Yorke. This particular night when Archibald had called in at 12:40 a.m., Sergeant Yorke told him to investigate a wild party on Powell Street in Vancouver's East End. Twenty minutes later Archibald phoned back to say the trouble was settled. The merrymakers were paying for a broken window, and the property owner wanted no further action taken.

Archibald should have called again at 1:40 a.m.. When he didn't Sergeant Yorke felt that some minor occurrence had kept him away from the call box. But when he still hadn't called an hour later Sergeant Yorke told Patrol Sergeant Walter Shirley to investigate. Another hour passed. Finally, Shirley reported no trace of the missing policeman. Yorke, now worried, directed six other men to search the lonely East End beat, and reported the matter to Deputy Chief McRae.

At daybreak, the Deputy was on the scene with four policemen. Later they were joined by Sergeant Dan Campbell and Detective Dick Levis. It was Levis' day off, but he was a friend of Archibald's and wanted to help.

Not until nine that morning did searchers get a lead. The manager of the Hastings Mill offices on Powell Street reported his premises broken into overnight. Sergeant Campbell and Detective Levis were detailed to investigate. They found that the office door had been jimmied and the office ransacked but nothing taken.

Then they checked outside of the building. At the front Campbell eyed the brush on a vacant lot across the street. He went over and shouted for Levis. Constable Archibald's body was lying face up behind a bush. The front of his blue tunic was bloodstained, beside him the blue helmet bearing the familiar maple leaf badge. Closer examination showed that he had been shot twice. Although his money and wallet appeared intact, his gun and flashlight were missing.

From the footprints round the body at least two other men had been present, and from the depressed appearance of the grass they must have been lying or sitting in concealment. Then Levis saw a piece of black cloth hanging on a nearby bush. It was a mask made of black satin, with two eye holes.

"I'll sure as hell find out where this came from," muttered Levis grimly, "and before nightfall."

Campbell, knowing Levis' reputation for digging up information along the waterfront, also knew it was no idle boast. "You'd better take Tisdale with you," he said.

As Campbell phoned in the news, Detectives Levis and Tisdale left for the waterfront haunts. Hour after hour they visited squatters' shacks, searched alleys, banged on doors and listened to a variety of surly denials. Finally, at Blackie Seymour's shack, their persistence brought results. Blackie, a swarthy giant, was in bed when they arrived just after noon. Rousing him, the experienced Levis noticed a hint of fear in his red-rimmed eyes.

"Get your pants on," he snapped, "then tell us where you were last night."

Blackie swore that he had never been out of the cabin all night. Tisdale took over the questioning while Levis searched the room. Flashlight in hand, he peered into the darkness of an empty drum-type heater, then shook out the contents of a cheap suitcase. Next he swept the light under the bed. A scrap of circular black cloth, shiny satin material, caught his attention. He suddenly realized that it was from one of the eye holes in the mask they had found near the murdered Constable Archibald. Levis looked closer and found its mate.

As he turned them over in his fingers he eyed Blackie. "Come on, Blackie, where were you last night?"

"Nowhere," whined Blackie.

"Who was here with you?"

"No one."

Levis wagged a finger in front of his nose. "Blackie, one of our men was killed on Powell Street early this morning, and no one is going to hold out on me!"

The ominous tone in Levis' voice changed Blackie's mind. He admitted there were three men with him in the cabin: Bill Hamilton, Frank Davis and Herman Clark. Davis and Clark were armed, one with a Smith and Wesson, the other with an Ivor Johnson. From their conversation he understood they had a case full of burglar's tools cached in the brush on Powell Street.

The four decided to pull a few stickups in the suburbs, then rob the Hastings Mill office. They were going to Shaughnessy by street car, but he and Hamilton got on the wrong car and never met the other two. They returned to the cabin and had a few drinks. Hamilton left and he turned in. He hadn't seen Clark or Davis since they left for Shaughnessy.

Levis jotted down descriptions of Blackie's companions, adding the information that Hamilton hung around the Senator Bar, and Clark and Davis had a room in the City Hotel on East Hastings. While Tisdale stayed with Blackie, Levis phoned Deputy Chief McRae. Before nightfall, Hamilton, Clark and Davis were in cells, but in different substations.

A fingerprint check showed that Clark was wanted for escaping from Folsom Prison in California where he had served two years of an 11-year sentence for armed robbery. His companion, Davis, also had a record.

He told police that he had been nowhere near Blackie's cabin the night before. Instead, he had stayed in North Vancouver, but couldn't remember the name of the man or the location of the house. He learned of the shooting when he met Clark in the morning and read the paper. This statement proved him a liar since Archibald's body was discovered at 9:30 a.m., long after the paper was on the streets.

Meanwhile Clark, wondering what was going on, also decided to talk. He backed up Blackie's story.

He said they were all at Blackie's place the night before where they got guns. Then he and Davis went to Shaughnessy. When they didn't meet up with Hamilton and Seymour, he and Davis retrieved the hidden tools and broke into the mill office. After Constable Archibald appeared they hid in the brush in the vacant lot. From there they watched the policeman check around then look up and down the street. He must have seen the glow of Davis' cigarette since he crossed the street, gun in one hand, flashlight in the other. When they were revealed in the flashlight's beam, they stood up, Davis holding a gun behind his back.

"What's your name?" asked Archibald. He never got an answer. Davis stepped back and fired three times.

He and Davis then fled, Clark continued. Two blocks away Davis suddenly remembered their tools. They ran back to get them and Davis took Archibald's gun and flashlight. Both were later thrown in a mudhole at Clark Drive and Hastings. Later that night they cached their tools and guns in a hollow stump on Inverness between 16th and 17th. The police later found all the articles.

Davis, meanwhile, had begun wondering what Clark was saying. He had also decided that his alibi about being in North Vancouver wasn't too convincing and changed his story. It agreed with everything that Clark said — with one radical difference. It was Clark who lit the cigarette in the brush and Clark who killed the policeman.

The Crown detained Hamilton and Blackie Seymour as material witnesses. A few months later Clark and Davis appeared before Mr. Justice Aulay Morrison. It was a curious courtroom drama. Each of the accused tried to put the other on the gallows.

Both were found guilty and executed at Oakalla in mid-April 1914.

If it was luck that gave Levis the break in the Clark and Davis case when he found the mask and matching material from the eye slits, the same fickle goddess frowned the following year. Late one night, chasing an armed killer, he paused in front of the man's East End bedroom door. No more dramatic scene was ever witnessed in B.C. police annals.

The terrified wife, afraid of the policeman killing her husband, was afraid also that her husband would kill a policeman. As she stood speechless by the bedroom door, the slim detective, gun in hand, eyed her. Then with one free hand he wordlessly pointed to the door, meaning: "Is he in there?"

Wearily, she nodded her head.

Levis motioned her aside. Then he charged. As he hit the door, the killer, crouched in the darkened room, fired both barrels of a shotgun.

Dick Levis left a wife, two boys and a girl.

It took a long time to find Levis' killer, but finally he was traced to Boston. He, too, died on the gallows at Oakalla.

# The Miner Who Died Eight Times

**Throughout his short life Robert Sproule was beset by misfortune. The final agony was being hanged for murder — even though he could well have been innocent.**

Like the last of the leaves falling around Victoria that morning of October 29, 1886, Robert Evans Sproule in the Hillside Jail realized that in minutes he, too, must fall — through a trap door, into oblivion.

Sproule was a sparsely built man of about 40, and as he sat on his steel-strap bunk, he occasionally clenched his hands. His eyes, deep

sunk with months of worry, showed a weariness, and the muscles at one side of his mouth twitched. From time to time a shudder shook his bowed shoulders.

Three other men were in the cell with him, men who had volunteered to keep him company in his final moments. They were men whose names Vancouver Islanders held in high esteem — William Webb Percival, J. H. Hawthornthwaite and Reverend Donald Fraser. Apart from these men Sproule was alone and friendless — a U.S. citizen who in the previous 11 months had been condemned to death seven times. Now, as footsteps broke the silence in the corridor, for the eighth time the noose beckoned. Reverend Fraser, reading from the Bible, closed his leather-bound book. Then Chief Jailer Muldoon swung open the heavy door: "Sproule, the time has arrived and the mandate of the law must be fulfilled."

Insofar as Canadian law was concerned, the trail that led Robert

Thomas Hammill, the claim jumper whom Sproule was accused of murdering.

Hillside Jail where Sproule had his death sentence postponed seven times. The man in the center of the group is Warden R. F. John and to his left is Head Gaoler William Muldoon who led Sproule to the gallows.

Evans Sproule to a condemned cell in Victoria's Hillside Jail started on the rocky slopes of Kootenay Lake's Galena Bay around 11 o'clock in the morning of June 1, 1885. Sproule had arrived on Kootenay Lake in 1882 when there were fewer than a dozen whites in the entire region. He and two companions staked four claims which they named the Kootenay Chief, the Comfort, the Ruby and the Blue Bell after the bluebells blooming amid the rocks.

At that time the mining laws stated that during the mining season from June 1 to October 31, claims could not be left unattended for more than three days without official permission. That autumn Sproule's companions left their claims before the October 31 deadline, but Sproule was determined to wait until the legal date. Unfortunately, his food ran out and he became ill. On October 25 he wrote a note explaining his problems and fastened it to a corner post of his Blue Bell claim. Then he left.

That summer, however, he hadn't been alone in staking claims. An Englishman called Thomas B. Hammill was busy staking claims for his employer, Captain John Ainsworth and his son, George, of a well established Oregon family wealthy from holdings in railroads and steamboats. When Sproule was forced to leave the claims six days ahead of the October 31 deadline, Hammill and his companions promptly staked them, Hammill taking the Blue Bell.

For Sproule, it wasn't his first experience with others taking what he felt was his property. In a grab for town lots in Pitcairn, Colorado, he had found himself involved in a maze of claims and counterclaims. Then in 1878 when he had stumbled on the rich Carbon Hill coal seam 30 miles east of Tacoma, ill-luck again dogged him. This time the County Auditor, with the connivance of two lawyers, falsified County records to swindle Sproule out of his claims. Infuriated, Sproule set fire to the Auditor's barn. As a consequence, a warrant was issued for his arrest and he fled to Canada. Now his claims on Kootenay Lake had been jumped.

In 1883 Sproule went to court to get the claims back. West Kootenay Justice of the Peace Edward Kelly ruled that Hammill's action was illegal and that Sproule's group still owned all the claims. The wealthy Ainsworths appealed.

In Victoria in March 1884, B.C.'s most famous Justice, Matthew Baillie Begbie, ruled that Sproule's companions had forfeited their claims by leaving early. Sproule, however, had attempted to stay but was forced to leave by circumstances. He could keep his claim. In giving his judgment, Begbie made it perfectly clear that he considered Hammill virtually a professional claim jumper who had been spying on Sproule all summer waiting for a chance to jump the Blue Bell.

After the court case, Sproule sold the Blue Bell to Dr. Wilbur Hendryx of the Kootenay Mining & Smelting Company. He then worked the claim for the Smelting Company. Thus on the morning of June 1, 1885, Sproule and three men: Charles Howes, and Adam and Charles Wolfe, were at work on the claim. Nearby, Hammill and his men were working the other three claims.

There was evident an air of tension, for Sproule had repeatedly said he would kill Hammill if he found him on his claim. This morning Hammill appeared and started sampling ore on the Blue Bell property. About 11 a.m. a rifle shot echoed round the surrounding hills. But the echo was to travel much farther than Kootenay Lake. It travelled westward across Canada to Ottawa, over the Atlantic to the Privy Council in London, and southward to the White House in Washington, D.C. It also summoned the population of Victoria to protest meetings and nearly split the legal unity of Canada.

On the hillside above Kootenay Lake that morning, however, few of the miners paid much attention to the shot. Or so they said later. It was Nick Velnoweth, on his way to lunch, who found Hammill lying on the side of the hill on the Blue Bell property. He had been shot in the back. In his agony he had beaten his face against the rocks until he was almost unrecognizable. Bending over the injured man, Velnoweth couldn't at first figure what was the matter with him. He hadn't heard a rifle shot.

"Keep your head — don't get excited," gasped Hammill through blood smeared lips. "Go and get some help."

Velnoweth scrambled over the rocky hillside to a bunkhouse and came back with a man. Together they carried the injured Hammill to one of the log shacks. Moments later he died.

One of the miners then rowed across the lake to Hot Springs Camp (now called Ainsworth) to get Provincial Constable Henry Anderson who arrived about 2 p.m. He was immediately aware that the miners were being very vague. He did learn that Sproule that morning had asked one of his miners, Adam Wolfe, for the loan of his rifle and some shells. Wolfe had thrown six shells on a bunk.

Some said they did not hear the shot at 11 a.m.; others said they heard it and thought someone was hunting. At midday, Wolfe sat down in the bunkhouse with his companions for lunch. Suddenly he noticed his rifle propped in the corner of the room and remarked: "Well, he brought it back."

He examined the gun, worked the bolt and extracted a spent cartridge case. "Pity he couldn't have cleaned it after he used it," was his remark. Then he added: "I'm going to keep this shell in case there's any trouble."

It seemed strange to Constable Anderson that the man who hadn't heard a shot, and didn't know a man had been killed, should have such an interest in the cartridge case. Sproule was absent during the Police Officer's visit, and enquiries for him produced evasive remarks. He'd left, but no one seemed to know when. He'd left by boat to cross the lake. At what time? No one was quite sure.

Eventually, Anderson found a man who'd seen Sproule leaving in a rowboat. He got into it at the lake edge carrying his own rifle, a Winchester. Just before he sat down, he worked the lever as if to put a shell in the breach.

Anderson asked Velnoweth if Hammill had told him who shot him.

"Never thought of it," said Velnoweth, "I was too excited. Besides, I figured he needed help quickly."

Maybe Hammill's answer wouldn't have added anything to the investigation. The bullet, fired from uphill, struck Hammill in the back, severing his spine. He probably never saw his assailant.

Thus far, Constable Anderson had learned that Hammill had been killed by a shot in the back and Sproule had left camp. There was bad blood between the two men. According to one story, later contradicted by another miner, Sproule had borrowed a gun in the morning and replaced it — a fired shell in it. He had left, taking his own gun. No one was sure when he left. As with many aspects of the murder, there are varying versions of what happened next. According to one, Anderson and an Indian helper set off in pursuit in a rowboat. They estimated that he was about seven miles ahead of them. After several hours they saw him, a speck in the distance. Relentlessly they followed Sproule 45 miles down the lake. With the wind whipping the lake surface into a nasty chop, Anderson was only a mile behind and gaining when Sproule finally turned his boat inshore. Landing among some boulders, he took his rifle and disappeared into the bush. There was no doubt in the policeman's mind that Sproule was in flight and that he would try to intercept a mountain trail that skirted the lake and would take him to the U.S. border.

On the fourth day in the woods, after Anderson and his helper had made camp, the Indian shot a bear for food. That evening as they sat by their campfire they heard twigs breaking nearby. Constable Anderson jumped to his feet, Winchester in hand. It was Sproule, a rifle under his arm. He walked into the clearing in time to see Anderson and hear the question: "Is your name Sproule?"

He admitted it was.

"Then," said Anderson, "You are just the man I'm looking for. Drop that gun."

They learned that Sproule, out of food, had heard the Indian's shot and headed for the sound.

The true story of the chase, however, is neither as colorful nor as dramatic. It was written by West Kootenay historian Edward L. Affleck whose massive research into West Kootenay history resulted in four excellent volumes called *The Kootenays in Retrospect*. In Volume Four, *Kootenay Lake* chronicles, is the following account:

"Anderson and a posse rowed a boat to the Outlet, and there picked up two canoes and Indian paddlers, who assisted in the pursuit of Sproule's boat. At a point on the lakeshore which was not connected by trail either to the Dewdney Trail or to the Fort Flatbow-Bonners Ferry Trail, Sproule's boat was found abandoned, apparently in good condition. Fighting rough weather. Anderson forthwith travelled up the lake and river to J. C. Rykert's custom house on the International Boundary. He there deployed his posse on either side of the Kootenay River, instructing them to patrol the 100-foot wide swath, now choked with undergrowth, which had been cut through the timber a quarter of a century before by the men making the boundary for the Boundary

Commission. A particularly sharp watch was kept at the point where the trail linking the Dewney Trail with Bonners Ferry crossed the clearing.

"Three days later, Sproule walked out of the bush near the clearing, was immediately arrested by Anderson, and detained in George Wallace Hall's cabin. He was then taken back up to the Blue Bell site where he was examined by Magistrate Arthur Vowell, who committed him to prison in New Westminster to await trial. On Chief Justice Begbie changing the trial venue, Sproule was moved to Victoria to await trial."

The case opened before Mr. Justice J. H. Gray at the Victoria Fall Assize early in December 1885. As the story unfolded the jury heard of the claim jumping, of the conflict between Hammill and Sproule, of the threats made by the accused, and of a bullet fired downhill that tore into Hammill's back to leave him writhing in agony on the ground.

Adam Wolfe gave his evidence of lending the gun and shells to Sproule on the morning of the killing. He was asked twelve times during the hearing why he had kept the fired shell, but had no convincing answer. Charlie Wolfe heard Sproule ask for the rifle, while another man heard Sproule threaten to kill Hammill. Both Adam and Charlie Wolfe were later to swear an affidavit that they had lied on the witness stand.

Tom Manning, engineer on the lakeboat *Reindeer*, held the jury's interest as he told of Constable Anderson and his prisoner getting aboard. Sproule walked up the gangplank first and stretched out his hand to a man called Rice as if he needed assistance. Manning felt sure something passed between the two, possibly a nugget, so he followed Rice along the deck. It was a page from a pocket notebook on which Sproule had written: "I am well satisfied that [Constable] Anderson knew that Thomas Hammill was going to jump the Blue Bell claim, as they were thick together. I am not allowed to communicate a word in writing that they cannot see.... They took all my money. They may confiscate the provisions that belong to the Kootenay Mining and Smelting Co., but I shall protest as they were invoiced to the company. Tell the company to send down men to work. I could not be on all the claims on the west side."

Sproule maintained that he wasn't fleeing when he left the Blue Bell. As Edward L. Affleck notes in *Kootenay Lake Chronicles*:

"There is no doubt but what suspicion fixed immediately upon Sproule as the murderer of Thomas Hammill, for he was the only one to leave the Blue Bell site on the morning of June 1, 1885, and he furthermore abandoned his boat, in good condition at an odd location on the lakeshore and took to the rough slopes above the lake. Sproule maintained that after advising his three-man crew of the work to be carried out on the Blue Bell claim during his absence, he had set out in a small skiff at 9:25 A.M. bound for Bonners Ferry and Kootenai Station, the latter point being Dr. Hendryx's headquarters for the Kootenay Mining & Smelting Company. His skiff he had abandoned for fear that it would be unseaworthy in the rough water which was blowing up. (A storm did blow up on June 1, severely hampering Anderson's efforts in the chase.) Sproule claimed further that he had no need to borrow Wolfe's rifle at any time, as his own which he brought away with him was in perfect working order. None of the Hammill party saw Sproule leave the Blue Bell site."

The court battle for Sproule's life involved two of B.C.'s most notable lawyers. Attorney-General A. B. Davie, who prosecuted, was to become B.C.'s Premier the next year. His brother, Theodore Davie who defended Sproule, became Premier in the 1890s.

Theodore Davie skillfully played up the question of the "Ainsworth Corporation" which had 750,000 acres of land staked and

GLORY HOLE
BLUEBELL MINE

employed scores of men to stake and maybe "jump" claims. He traced Hammill's career as a professional claim jumper and produced as witnesses men like James Hobkirk who knew Hammill as a claim jumper in Colorado in 1879-80.

"Sproule never fled from the law," said Davie. "Most of the time he was travelling down the lake he was trolling. Perhaps," he concluded, "Indians shot Hammill."

He turned an exploratory glance on the Wolfe brothers and their evasive answers. Why did Adam Wolfe make such a fuss about the spent cartridge when he didn't know a man had been shot?

When the evidence was in, Mr. Justice Gray addressed the jury for five hours. The jury deliberated for five hours and were unable to agree. They went back for another hour. Finally at 11 p.m. on December 7, 1885, they returned with their verdict: "Guilty, but with a recommendation to mercy."

Defence counsel Davie wanted the jury polled, but the Attorney-General objected.

Above: Across the lake from the site of the Blue Bell was the first community on Kootenay Lake, first called Hot Springs Camp then changed to today's Ainsworth. It is shown in the early 1890s. Here Hammill's death was reported to Constable Anderson.

Opposite page: Rykert's Custom House where Constable Anderson's patrol captured Sproule, and the southerly face of the Blue Bell Mine. The Glory Hole leads into the galleries below.

Sproule was thereupon sentenced to die on January 5. Events proved otherwise. As Sproule sat in his Hillside cell awaiting execution, people in Victoria started to take sides. From a murmur it became angry debate. Points in the case were rehashed and opinion favored Sproule, not only in B.C. but throughout North America.

Theodore Davie argued before B.C.'s Supreme Court for a reversal of judgment. In response, the Court granted Sproule a reprieve until April 6. It was only four months to live, but it was something. Davie had argued that Mr. Justice Gray had no jurisdiction to hear the case, objecting to a trial in Victoria for an offence committed in West Kootenay.

Sproule, in the meantime, received no visitors, no letters. A sad and alien figure, he knew only that Queen Victoria was going to hang him on April 6. Nearer drew the ominous date until death was only 24 hours away. The afternoon before his execution, the Chief Jailer told him that an order had come through reprieving him to May 6. Another month! Apparently the additional time was necessary for the Minister of Justice at Ottawa to study the case. He did. His edict was that Sproule should hang on May 6 as scheduled.

In the meantime, the wind of public opinion in Victoria was reaching storm force. On May 1, a week before the execution date, a mass protest meeting was held in Victoria's City Hall, with Mayor Fell in the chair. Chief reason for the protest was the jury's recommendation to mercy. Had it been taken into account? No. It had been totally ignored. In impassioned tones Mayor Fell said he wouldn't hang a dog on the evidence that convicted Sproule, the jury was misled by witnesses who perjured themselves, and the judge charged too strongly against the prisoner.

He brought up the question of Crown witnesses Charles and Adam Wolfe. Charles had filed an affidavit admitting that they had lied in court. "An affidavit has been filed," charged the Mayor, "that they perjured themselves at the trial. They were to get $500 plus expenses to give their evidence."

The evidence against Sproule was circumstantial only, the case made even more tenuous since two of the Crown's witnesses had admitted that they lied. In addition, several of the jurors swore affidavits that they had agreed to the guilty verdict only because they had been assured that with their recommendation for mercy, Sproule would not be given the death penalty. An even more damning affidavit against the Crown's case was reported by Edward L. Affleck in his already mentioned *Kootenay Lake Chronicles:*

"Charles Howes [one of the workmen at the Blue Bell] did not testify at Sproule's trial, but following the trial he filed an affidavit in Idaho to the effect that Sproule had left the Blue Bell site in his boat about 10 A.M. after advising Howes of his impending departure. Howes also stated that Sproule could not have left his cabin to shoot Hammill without being seen, and that Sproule had not borrowed Adam Wolfe's rifle that morning. Howes further stated that Constable Henry Anderson had advised him and the Wolfe brothers in Sandpoint in October, 1885 that rewards would be forthcoming to those who could offer up evidence against Sproule at the trial."

In view of this obvious miscarriage of justice, it wasn't surprising that the Victoria meeting ended with a resolution that there should be a searching enquiry into the whole case. Meantime, local U.S. Consul Colonel Stevens was making representations to his government, with a hint of new evidence that would mean a new trial. Some of the jurors had made a declaration that their guilty vote was filed without the knowledge that capital punishment was involved.

Three days before the third execution date, word came from the Deputy Minister of Justice at Ottawa. The result was another 30-day stay of execution, the fourth. Then on June 4 came further word from Ottawa that the judgment of the Supreme Court of Canada might not be known before the end of the week. Therefore it would be better to postpone the execution date until July 6.

Finally came word on June 20 that the Supreme Court of Canada had decided that Sproule's trial was null and void. He should have been tried in West Kootenay where the crime occurred. As well as being complete confirmation of defence counsel Theodore Davie's argument, it meant that the prisoner would be discharged.

But where? In Victoria? Or by the Supreme Court at Ottawa? On July 6, the day Sproule was to have hanged, there arrived in Victoria a writ of habeas corpus issued by the Supreme Court of Canada ordering the delivery forthwith to Ottawa of Robert Evans Sproule. But the unfortunate Sproule remained in jail. The B.C. Government, apparently determined to hang him, announced that it was ignoring the writ of habeas corpus. It was going to appeal to the Privy Council in London!

"The Jurisdiction of Canada's Supreme Court in Jeopardy!" screamed headlines in Eastern papers. Meantime, in his bleak cell which had neither light nor water, Sproule learned that he had been again respited, this time until August 19. Death had paused for a look at him and moved on for the sixth time.

On August 7, lawyer Davie made a motion before Mr. Justice Henry in Ottawa to have Sproule discharged, with a rider that Sproule's attendance at Ottawa be dispensed with. His Lordship granted the request that Sproule be set free.

Incredibly, B.C.'s Attorney-General disobeyed the ruling, even though the public now generally believed that Sproule had not been given a fair trial. When Sheriff McMillan at Victoria received the Supreme Court's writ for Sproule's summary release, he ignored it.

"He is not to decide the validity of these documents," rapped Mr. Justice Henry when he heard of the Sheriff's action, adding: "Certainly no local Sheriff is going to usurp judicial authority."

With Provincial and Dominion Governments now enmeshed in a legal battle, Sproule's August 19 date with the hangman was again postponed. Death again had lingered at his cell but passed on.

On September 1 the Sproule case opened at Ottawa before a specially summoned sitting of the Supreme Court of Canada. Representing the B.C. Government were three prominent lawyers, while Davie and two others fought for Sproule. The Supreme Court by a majority decision ruled that Sproule's trial had been constitutionally correct. The result was that Sproule was sentenced to hang on October 1. It was the seventh death sentence for the unfortunate American.

Once more lawyer Theodore Davie fought to save Sproule. A week later he appeared before Mr. Justice Gray at Victoria, arguing for Sproule's reprieve until he could take the appeal to the Privy Council in London.

The motion was opposed by B.C.'s Attorney-General. Said Judge Gray, in effect: "The federal executive, having considered the matter and denied a reprieve, a B.C. judge can go no further."

"By interfering now," he added, "I am assuming a power entirely beyond anything conceded to a judge. Therefore, I must decline to interfere."

What next? Sproule was to hang in 10 days. One rumor was that the U.S. State Department had been in touch with Ottawa. In fact there is a letter on record from Secretary of State Thomas F. Bayard to Franklin Sproule, the condemned man's father in Maine. In the letter Bayard counseled "…we will enquire into the matter. In the meantime rest assured that Canadian authority will no doubt take every possible action in order that justice may be done."

Unfortunately for Sproule, the B.C. Government seemed more interested in hanging him than in re-examining the case for possible injustice.

The British Government in London had also been asking questions about the Sproule case and possibly passed along the suggestion that Sproule might be adjudged insane. In any event, Doctors Hanington and Milne of Victoria were appointed "a commission de lunatico inquirendo." It was no good. After their examination the doctors reported that Sproule "is of sound mind and good judgment and fully accountable."

Theodore Davie by this time was looking for other legal angles. There seemed to be none. However, two days before the scheduled hanging the fighting defence counsel wired the Minister of Justice to postpone the execution to allow an appeal to the Privy Council in London. The Minister replied: "The law must be carried out. Sproule will be executed October 1, whether he appeals or not."

Because of this continued dance with death, Sproule ate little of the prison food which was essentially bread and gruel. Death had now passed by six times. Perhaps, however, the postponements were working for him since many people felt that the mental torture he had undergone was alone reason to justify commutation.

Then, incredibly, on the afternoon before his scheduled execution, the jailer again brought word of a reprieve — the seventh. Sproule would now hang on Friday, October 29.

"The coffin has been made, the rope is ready, and the scaffold erected," wrote editor D. W. Higgins in the Victoria *Colonist*. "And a telegram comes from Ottawa a mere 16 hours before the hanging…. It's a refinement of cruelty to hang him now."

The smelter at Pilot Bay built to process Blue Bell ore. The venture quickly failed and today all that remain are the two crumbling stacks.

The Blue Bell Mine and the community of Riondel in the 1960s. Although the ore body is now exhausted, the community survives as a retirement center.

The reason for the last-minute delay was that the U.S. State Department and the British Colonial Office were getting bombarded with disquieting rumors about a claim jumping case in B.C. Would Canada's Government take a second look at the case? Apparently Ottawa did, and on October 27 came the answer: Sproule would hang on October 29 as scheduled, the eighth death sentence.

When October 28 dawned in Ottawa, still one more interested person was to be heard from. He was Mayor Fell of Victoria who had paid his own expenses to go to Ottawa and present a petition from Victoria citizens. He didn't know much about protocol, but in a quick series of office-to-office conferences he found men who would lead him to cabinet ministers. Finally, in late afternoon, one minister was so impressed with the fervour of Victoria's Mayor that he got him an interview with Prime Minister John A. Macdonald.

In brief, emotion-packed phrases, Fell told Canada's Prime Minister that a pardon or commutation was the hope of those he represented at the coast. It was no use. The law had to have its way. Fell, deeply despondent, returned to his hotel room to await the next train.

On October 29, 1886, citizens who picked up their Victoria *Colonist* found the lead editorial headed "The Final Act." It went on to say: "Before these lines shall have reached the majority of our readers Robert Evans Sproule, whether guilty or guiltless of the murder of which he was convicted, will be beyond human aid....

"If he was guilty," the editorial continued, "then in deference to contrary opinion he should have had commutation."

While *Colonist* carriers were collecting their papers that morning, Sproule woke in his jail cell about 5 a.m. He seemed to have slept well, but there was still that haunted, wistful look about his sunken eyes. More noticeable than ever was an incessant twitch at the muscles of his mouth.

At 8 o'clock the Head Jailer opened the cell door and summoned him to his last walk. Sproule went into the yard with a firm step, blinked at the morning light and perhaps at the sight of some 20 spectators. He noticed Sheriff McMilland and the black-masked executioner, then climbed the steps to the scaffold with Reverend Donald Fraser. The silence was oppressive as the spectators below stood with heads uncovered. Turning to the Jailer, Sproule asked, "Can I speak to the Sheriff?"

"You can."

To the Sheriff he said: "Mr. Sheriff, you haven't read the death warrant yet."

"No, it isn't necessary." said the Sheriff.

"Can I speak a few words further?" asked Sproule in a low tone.

"Yes, if you wish," was the answer.

There was silence as seconds ticked by. Sproule cleared his throat and, looking down at the strained faces below him, began:

"My friends, this is a very solemn situation, to pass out of the world in such a condition. I trust this will be an example and warning to all who commit sin. The charge that has been preferred against me

Those involved in the Sproule case included A. E. Davie, top left. He was B.C.'s Attorney-General, seemingly determined to hang Sproule. Davie himself was fated for a short life, dying in 1889 at 43.

Theodore Davie, the Attorney-General's brother, top right, used every legal recourse in his determined attempt to save Sproule.

Victoria's Mayor Fell, below, paid his own way to Ottawa to plead with Prime Minister John A. Macdonald to at least commute Sproule's sentence.

Editor D. W. Higgins, bottom right, wrote that "It's a refinement of cruelty to hang him now."

was wrong. I was not guilty of the crime of which I was accused. Eight witnesses who came to Victoria bore false witness against me, which led to my conviction. They know as well as I the wrong they have perpetrated. I have nothing further to say, only, goodbye to you all."

The executioner slipped forward and tightened the rope around Sproule's neck. Feeling it tighten as he looked at the sky, he yelled, "Don't strangle me."

Quietly, the Head Jailer went down the steps, leaving Sproule standing erect, hat in one hand, handkerchief in the other. Reverend Fraser intoned a prayer. The executioner pulled a cap over Sproule's eyes and the Sheriff gave a brief inclination of his head. The masked executioner pulled the lever. A drop of eight feet resulted in instantaneous death reported Coroner Dr. John Helmcken. The man who had died mentally on seven previous occasions was officially dead.

After his death, the Sproule case continued to agitate the public. There was comment, editorial and otherwise, some of it mild appraisal, some scorching criticism. The *New York Tribune's* editorial four days later charged that "the defendant was the victim of a foul conspiracy … an innocent man has been murdered … shamefully put to death because he was a citizen of the U.S."

In milder tone Canadian opinion could be summed up in Mayor Fell's parting remark to Sir John A. Macdonald: "There is something about this case I cannot understand."

Meanwhile, during the legal jousting the Kootenay Mining & Smelting Company had acquired all the claims surrounding the Blue Bell. In 1891 the Company decided to build a smelter to process the ore. It was built on Lighthouse Point some eight miles from the mine. To service the smelter, the townsite of Pilot Bay appeared and by 1895 some 3,000 tons of silver-lead bullion were shipped. But the smelter wasn't destined to survive. The ore had a low silver and high lead content and operating costs were high. Pilot Bay Smelter shut down in 1896, with the concentrator used sporadically until 1906. Thereafter the community of Pilot Bay withered, two crumbling brick stacks now the only evidence of its existence. Was the Blue Bell fated to destroy all of those who became involved with it?

The property was purchased in 1905 by a French group headed by Count Edouard Riondel. This venture proved unsuccessful and they left. In 1924 S. S. Fowler and B. L. Eastman became the new owners. They proved no more successful than the French and in 1931 sold out to the giant Consolidated Mining & Smelting Company at Trail. Backed by the massive resources of this giant Canadian Pacific Railway firm, the Blue Bell at last seemed destined for success. It was — but not for another 20 years — over 60 years after Hammill jumped it.

In the early 1950s it started producing some 250,000 tons of lead-zinc ore a year. The nearby community of Riondel soon had a population of 600 and a prosperous looking future. Had the jinx of the Blue Bell been broken? It appeared so since the ore proved to be one of the most economical low grade galena deposits ever mined. Over the next 20 years it yielded some 5 million tons, but then was exhausted. The mine closed again, this time permanently.

The community of Riondel survived, but as a retirement rather than a mining center. It contains a memorial to Thomas Hammill, but nothing to commemorate Sproule. The Hammill memorial was erected by Cominco when they had to disturb his grave. The wooden slab which stood at the head of the grave is now in Nelson's Museum, the inscription faithfully reproduced on Cominco's impressive monument. It reads:

---

THOMAS HAMMILL

ASSASSINATED

JUNE 1, 1885

AGE 30 YEARS

---

Old-time prospectors, however, were not impressed. As the late David Scott and Edna Hanic note in their book, *NELSON: Queen City of the Kootenays:*

"Cominco had every right to expect old-timers to be delighted with their fine memorial to Hammill, but instead, Kootenay prospectors screamed, 'Who wants a memorial to that stinking claim jumper?'"

As for Sproule, even in death misfortune refused to release him. He wanted to be buried in U.S. soil, so his body was put in a plain coffin. But no one claimed him. No friends, no relatives appeared. He was buried in the jail yard on a hill top. A few years after his death the jail was demolished. Today it is the site of the S. J. Willis Junior High School, Sproule's burial plot unknown.

But even being buried in foreign soil in a unmarked grave wasn't the last of Sproule's misfortune. A few days after his execution came word that in his native Maine he had won a long standing legal suit which today would be the equivalent of over $1 million.

But the most cruel aspect of Sproule's buffeting by fate is that he could well have been innocent. As the November 4, 1886, issue of the *New York Tribune* commented:

"The hanging of Robert Sproule at Victoria, B.C. entails a fearful responsibility on the Canadian government. Evidence of Sproule's innocence is so strong as to have convinced the public that he was wrongly convicted."

**FRONT COVER**
Throughout the nearly century-long era of the B.C. Provincial Police, horses and dogs served the force. The cover photos are of Constable D. A. Jobling and his trail mate, Malamute, photographed at Dawson Creek by Corporal J. C. Sweeney, and Constable Dick Meadows at Oliver in 1933.

PHOTO CREDITS
B.C. Provincial Archives: 4-5, 8, 12-13, 17, 20-21, 23, 24, 30, 34, 36-37, 46, 47, 50, 52-53, 56, 57, 66-67, 81, 83, 86-87, 90, 96, 108, 113, 116, 126-127, 132, 133, 137, 139; B.C. Provincial Museum: 81; Clark, Cecil: 2, 5, 9, 34-35, 50, 56, 86; Glenbow-Alberta Institute: 102; National Museums of Canada: 79; Public Archives, Canada: 70, 82, 83; Shoulder Strap: 8, 12, 13, 15, 17, 26, 31, 75; Tourism B.C.: 118-119, 137; Vancouver City Archives: 61, 63; Vancouver Police Museum: 105, 122; Vancouver Public Library: 40-41, 72, 100-101.

Copyright © 1989 Cecil Clark

**CANADIAN CATALOGUING IN PUBLICATION DATA**

Clark, Cecil, 1899-
  B.C. Provincial Police stories

ISBN 0-919214-74-6 (v.1). — ISBN
0-919214-75-4 (v.2)

1. Crime and criminals — British Columbia — History. I. Title.
HV6809.B7C53 1986    364.1'09711    C86-091097.0

HERITAGE HOUSE PUBLISHING COMPANY LTD.     PRINTING HISTORY
Box 1228, Station A, Surrey. B.C. V3S 2B3     First Edition — 1989
                                             Second Printing — 1993
Printed in Canada.

# A selection of other HERITAGE HOUSE titles:

### The PIONEER DAYS IN BRITISH COLUMBIA Series
Every article is true, many written or narrated by those who, 100 or more years ago, lived the experiences they relate. Each volume contains 160 pages in large format magazine size (8½ x 11), four-color covers, some 60,000 words of text and over 200 historical photos, many published for the first time.

*A continuing Canadian best seller in three volumes which have sold over 75,000 copies. Each volume, $12.95*

### WHITE SLAVES OF THE NOOTKA
On March 22, 1803, while anchored in Nootka Sound on the West Coast of Vancouver Island, the *Boston* was attacked by "friendly" Nootka Indians. Twenty-five of her 27 crew were massacred, their heads "arranged in a line" for survivor John Jewitt to identify. Jewitt and another survivor became 2 of 50 slaves owned by Chief Maquina, never knowing what would come first — rescue or death.

*The account of their ordeal, published in 1815, remains remarkably popular. New Western Canadian edition, well illustrated. 128 pages. $9.95*

### THE DEATH OF ALBERT JOHNSON: Mad Trapper of Rat River
Albert Johnson in 1932 triggered the greatest manhunt in Canada's Arctic history. In blizzards and numbing cold he was involved in four shoot-outs, killing one policeman and gravely wounding two other men before being shot to death.

*This revised, enlarged edition includes photos taken by "Wop" May, the legendary bush pilot whose flying skill saved two lives during the manhunt. Another Canadian best seller. $7.95*

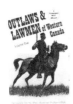

### OUTLAWS AND LAWMEN OF WESTERN CANADA
These true police cases prove that our history was anything but dull. Chapters in 160-page Volume Three, for instance, include Saskatchewan's Midnight Massacre, The Yukon's Christmas Day Assassins, When Guns Blazed at Banff, and Boone Helm — The Murdering Cannibal.

*Each of the three volumes in this Canadian best seller series is well illustrated with maps and photos, with four-color photos on the covers. Volume One, $8.95; Volume Two, $8.95; Volume Three, $9.95*

### B.C. PROVINCIAL POLICE STORIES: Mystery and Murder from the Files of Western Canada's First Lawmen
The B.C. Police, born in 1858, were the first lawmen in Western Canada. During their 90 years of service they established a reputation as one of the most progressive police forces in North America. All cases in these best selling titles are reconstructed from archives and police files.
Volume One: 16 chapters, many photos, 128 pages. $9.95
Volume Two: 22 chapters, many photos, 144 pages. $9.95
Volume Three: 23 chapters, many photos, 160 pages. $12.95

### B.C. BACKROADS
This best selling series contains complete information from Vancouver through the Fraser Canyon to Cache Creek, east to Kamloops country and north to the Cariboo. Also from Vancouver to Bridge River-Lillooet via Whistler. Each book contains mile-by-mile route mileage, history, fishing holes, wildlife, maps and photos.

*Volume One — Garibaldi to Bridge River Country-Lillooet. $9.95*
*Volume Three — Junction Country: Boston Bar to Clinton. $9.95*
*Thompson-Cariboo: Highways, byways, backroads. $4.95*

### An Explorer's Guide: MARINE PARKS OF B.C.

To tens of thousands of boaters, B.C.'s Marine Parks are as welcome and convenient as their popular highway equivalents. This guide includes anchorages and onshore facilities, trails, picnic areas, campsites, history and other information. In addition, it is profusely illustrated with color and black and white photos, maps and charts.
*Informative reading for boat owners from runabouts to cabin cruisers. 200 pages $12.95.*

---

## GO FISHING WITH THESE BEST SELLING TITLES

---

### HOW TO CATCH SALMON — BASIC FUNDAMENTALS

The most popular salmon book ever written. Information on trolling, rigging tackle, most productive lures, proper depths, salmon habits, downriggers, where to find fish, and much more.
*Sales over 130,000. 176 pages. $5.95*

### HOW TO CATCH SALMON — ADVANCED TECHNIQUES

The most comprehensive advanced salmon fishing book available. Over 200 pages crammed full of how-to-tips and easy-to-follow diagrams. Covers all popular salmon fishing methods: mooching, trolling with bait, spoons and plugs, catching giant chinook, and a creel full of other information.
*A continuing best seller. 192 pages. $11.95*

**HOW TO CATCH CRABS**: How popular is this book? This is the 11th printing, with sales over 90,000. $4.95

**HOW TO CATCH BOTTOMFISH**: Revised and expanded. $5.95

**HOW TO CATCH SHELLFISH**: Updated 4th printing. 144 pages. $3.95

**HOW TO CATCH TROUT** by Lee Straight, one of Canada's top outdoorsmen. 144 pages. $5.95

**HOW TO COOK YOUR CATCH**: Cooking seafood on the boat, in a camper or at the cabin. 8th printing. 192 pages. $4.95

### FLY FISH THE TROUT LAKES

with Jack Shaw
Professional outdoor writers describe the author as a man "who can come away regularly with a string when everyone else has been skunked." In this book, he shares over 40 years of studying, raising and photographing all forms of lake insects and the behaviour of fish to them.
*Written in an easy-to-follow style. 96 pages. $8.95*

### SALMON FISHING BRITISH COLUMBIA: Volumes One and Two

Since B.C. has some 7,000 miles of coastline, a problem to its 400,000 salmon anglers is where to fish. These books offer a solution. Volume One includes over 100 popular fishing holes around Vancouver Island. Volume Two covers the Mainland Coast from Vancouver to Jervis Inlet. Both include maps, gear to use, best times, lures and a tackle box full of other information.
*Volume One — Vancouver Island. $9.95*
*Volume Two — Mainland Coast: Vancouver to Jervis Inlet. $11.95*

---

**Heritage House books are sold throughout Western Canada. If not available at your bookstore you may order direct from Heritage House, Box 1228, Station A, Surrey, B.C. V3S 2B3. Payment can be by cheque or money order but add 7 per cent for the much hated GST. Books are shipped postpaid.**